A Month
at the
Brickyard

A Month at the Brickyard

THE INCREDIBLE INDY 500

★★★★★★★★★★★★★★★★★★★★★★★★★★★★★★★★

Sonny Kleinfield

★

HOLT, RINEHART and WINSTON • New York

Published simultaneously in Canada by Holt, Rinehart and Winston of Canada, Limited.

Library of Congress Cataloging in Publication Data

Kleinfield, Sonny.
  A month at the brickyard.

    1. Indianapolis Speedway Race. I. Title.
GV1033.5.I55K57   796.7′2′0680977252   76–47878
ISBN 0–03–017711–1

First Edition

Printed in the United States of America

10 9 8 7 6 5 4 3 2 1

TO THE MEMORY OF MY FATHER

Acknowledgments

I would like to acknowledge my appreciation to
Johnny Parsons and the members of his team—
particularly Tassi Vatis, Bill Finley, and John Barnes—
for their courtesy and willing cooperation.
I am also indebted to the management of the
Indianapolis Motor Speedway for its generosity.
Finally, and most of all,
I wish to express my gratitude to Bernice Mosesson,
who was there during the long days and nights.

A Month
at the
Brickyard

★★★★★★★★★★★★★★

B eyond the steel stands lining the track, the crowd begins to build. It spills onto the road. Pigeons wheel overhead. A couple of plump men are already debating who the winner will be. "He will too win." "Nah." A knot of teen-agers is further back; a radio, slung over one shoulder, is pounding out raunchy rock music. They are whooping it up. Their voices reach like claws to the furthest part of the crowd. "Unnnh-hunh! Unnnh-hunh!" It is a cool morning with no breeze to speak of. Inside, engines whine, hammers clank, mechanics are crouched over suspensions. At the very front of the line, a stringy man with a turkey throat is stooped over the steering wheel of his van, the sides of which are tattooed with every imaginable racing decal. His name—Larry Bisceglia —is also painted on the sides. A retired auto rebuilder in his seventies, he got into town a month ago, trundling in from Long Beach, California. He'll be first through the gates, adding to his legend. This will make it twenty-eight straight years. He says he does it to do it.

The stunted skyline of Indianapolis—a city of a million people surrounded by the flat fields of the Midwest—is visible behind him, above a view of adult book stores, gas stations, drive-in burgers. Traffic is bad. All over town, store windows are done up in checkered flags, there

1

are race specials, and the radio and television channels all offer shows featuring interviews with racing drivers. A racing movie is playing at a local drive-in. Signs propped outside motels read, WELCOME RACE FANS, WELCOME VALVOLINE, WELCOME CHAMPION. Big racing tires tilt together inside the lobbies. A radio commercial says, "If you're an avid race fan, come on over and get your hardware at Bill's. That's right. If you need hardware, make a pit stop at Bill's." Cars and trucks keep dragging in. The sky is cloudless. It is Saturday, the eighth of May, the first day of practice for the Indianapolis 500.

Down toward the first turn, Larry "Boom Boom" Cannon and his crew shove their race car onto the pit apron. Bands are pressing down the straightaway; the air rings with the smack of cymbals and high-collared drums. Cannon is trying to be the first man on the track. Being first out is not important in itself, but last year, when Cannon was one of the last men on the track, he never made the race. He figures being first this year will change his luck. Cannon is the recorder of deeds for Vermilion County, Illinois. A short while ago, he ran for state senator but lost. In his words, "the people lost."

Slumped in his car, engulfed by a gauntlet of press people, cameramen, the morbidly curious, Cannon is warned by an official not to go faster than 180 miles an hour today. His car owner—a tall, spare man—stands beside the car. Cannon says to him, "Will you pay the fine if I break the speed limit?"

The man looks away for a long moment. He finds an answer: "Yeah, if you run 200." If Cannon ran 200 miles per hour, he would shatter the track record.

Fifteen minutes to go. Fourteen. "Gimme my hat," Cannon says. He settles a black helmet over his hair, tugs on gloves. Eleven. Ten minutes, and the pace car makes a final inspection of the track. The track passes. Cannon's car is started. The engine catches with a throaty thrum. Its roar cuts up the spring air. A stammer of flashbulbs. Clapping crackles through the stands. Can-

2

non lurches onto the track. Everyone's eyes glued on him, he makes a lap. Suspense: the crowd waits. Stopwatches are consulted. Speed: 43 miles per hour.

In one of the small garages where the racing cars are quartered, Bill Finley, a slightly potbellied man with carroty side-whiskers, nearly fifty, is attempting to fit the hood over the engine of a car. It won't fit. "I swear this son of a bitch is pregnant on me," he says. He draws on a cigarette. Looking on is the owner of the car, a millionaire from New York. His name is Tassi Vatis, but people refer to him as "The Greek." John Barnes, a muscular man in his mid-twenties, is draped over the front of the car, half-disappeared into its innards. Finley hacks away some of the hood with a pair of cutters and tries again. It still won't fit. People come by to say hello, to talk, to stare, to look at the car. The car is white with a wide pink stripe and a narrower black one running the length of the left side. The number 93 is on the nose. Plastered on the side are the words "Ayr-Way WIRE Racing Team." Ayr-Way is a local shopping center chain; WIRE is a local country and western music station. The name of the driver shows up in black lettering, Johnny Parsons. Finley, the car's chief mechanic, massages his scalp. "What in God's name do I have to do to make this bugger fit?"

"Have you considered a smaller car?" Johnny Parsons says.

A crew man named Shorty Harrison, a plump man who looks vaguely like a stubbed-out cigar, is down on his knees smoothing decal numbers on a side of the car. "Now remember, Shorty," Finley says. "The 9 goes before the 3."

"Let me write that down," Shorty says.

Many of the other garages at this early hour on the first day are locked tight. Some gape emptily. The opening days of practice at the big track are a sort of scrambled homecoming. The cars have descended on Indianapolis

3

from all directions. Drivers, mechanics, crew helpers, owners, and sponsors are re-forming their teams, setting up their cars, and mapping out routines for the month. Big vans, painted up gaily, are chugging into the garage area, and out of their backs shining racers slide down wooden boards and then on into their stalls. The crewmen are petting and hugging the cars just like the trainers do the horses at the Kentucky Derby. Racing people are gypsies, hopscotching from track to track in search of gold and glory. Indianapolis is where the biggest dreams are dreamed. A mood prevails of people coming together for a collective celebration—a civic testimonial or class reunion. Everybody is saying hello to people they have not seen in a while, and everybody looks good.

"The first day's always a pleasant one," Tassi Vatis says. "Everybody's got his hopes up. This place can make you rich and famous in a single afternoon. Every race car owner wants to believe. The first day, we all believe we're going to win."

A crewman from another car toddles in, looks around. "Boy, that car of yours, it isn't much, that car."

"It'll outrun yours in second gear," Finley says.

"Doubtful. Quite doubtful."

"Tell us about it in Victory Lane."

Technical inspection is about to start. Three men with authority written all over their faces, officials of the United States Auto Club (USAC), the governing body for the race, shamble into the garage. The car has yet to turn a lap. Sweated over for much of a year, it has been saved for this race. A smorgasbord of some five thousand parts, some no bigger than a match head, the race car is a stumpy-nosed contraption that looks like a giant mosquito or a big doorstop. There's no roof on it. At the front are two small spoilers, and at the rear is a big wing. The spoilers and wing are both like upside-down airplane wings. They squash the car down onto the track, helping traction. A giant eight-hundred-horsepower Drake-Offenhauser engine—developed just for auto racing—

billows out of the rear. The engine is turbocharged, which causes it to emit a high-pitched whine. Like a vacuum cleaner, the turbocharger sucks air in and shoots it back through the engine, pumping up the power. The car is about fifteen feet long, nine feet wide, three feet high. It gets around 1.8 miles to the gallon.

One of the inspectors speaks over Finley's shoulder. "Bill, you call this a car?"

"Uh, would you believe a toaster?"

"Sounds more like it."

The inspectors poke into joints, measure the size of the engine, scratch down dimensions. There are shouts back and forth from the men, jokes, announcements, challenges. Inspection takes not more than an hour and a half.

As the men take their leave, Finley says with a smile, "Well, we duped them again."

The crew pushes number 93 to another area of the complex of garages to have the fuel tank checked. Forty gallons is the limit, a way to keep down the fiery wrecks that are common in the sport. The cars run on methanol, which is wood alcohol, because it delivers greater engine power and it's less liable to ignite than gasoline. Winding around the roadway, the crew moves past what look like miniature farm tractors tugging race cars. The tractors are connected to the cars by hunks of rope. Limping along, the cars remind one of sick Plymouths being yanked off the turnpike. Number 93 is brought to a stop in front of an island of two fuel pumps.

"Hey, you got four wheels on this one?" a lantern-jawed attendant says.

"Yeah," Finley says. "I'm improving all the time."

"Next thing you know, you'll put a motor in."

"What the hell's a motor?"

The tank size is found to be legal, and the car is taken to be weighed on a Revere electronic scale, a twenty-five-thousand-dollar marvel that can weigh a quarter as much as a Mack truck. On a giant digital readout that looks like the face of an enormous clock radio, the car number and total weight light up. A car can't run if it comes in at less than fifteen hundred pounds. Car number 93: fifteen hundred and thirty pounds.

"About the same as my wife," Finley snorts.

So far, thirteen cars have taken to the track, a lot of action for the first day. The cars hurry down the straights and around the corners, trying to cut fractional seconds off lap times. The fastest lap of all is run by Mario Andretti, a speed of 178.077. Enough to miss the starting lineup. For being the fastest of the day, Andretti wins two free dinners at the Classic Motor Lodge. Another driver roars out in a brand-new car, brand-new engine, steps on it, and watches as the engine explodes and rains parts over hundreds of feet of asphalt. Drivers call it "losing your lunch." There is nothing to do about a lost lunch but to buy a new one.

An hour before the track closes for the day, the crew eases number 93 out of the garage to fire up the engine and get it ready to run some laps. The engine coughs, sputters, catches. "Oh, damn," Finley says. A valve is dripping fuel, it will have to be replaced. "It was too much to expect to fire that son of a bitch and just go racing," he says. The engine shuts down and the crew shoves the car back into its stall. Finley and Barnes start to work on it.

★★★★★★★★★★★★★★★★

Downtown, Sixteenth Street rises to the White River and then cuts straight as a plumb line past a strip of bars, car washes, peep shows, 500 Auto Parts, 500 Shopping Center, 500 Bowling, 500 Pizza. Nudging above it all in the deadening heat is the old Speedway. Since 1909, men have been driving cars fast around it. A tract of five hundred and fifty-nine parklike acres, it actually hunkers in a jumble of houses and low buildings fittingly called the town of Speedway. Speedway claims fifteen thousand people but no mayor; a part-time board of trustees runs it. A featureless town. The dominant structures along the road are the billboards, mounted high above the buildings like huge kites. Shaped like a tremendous welcome mat, the track is two and a half miles around, its long straightaways are five-eighths of a mile long, the short ones one-eighth, the turns one-quarter. A cement retaining wall that delineates the circumference has been scarred all over by race cars flogging against it. Once the track's surface was all bricks (they still call it "The Brickyard"), but now the Speedway sports a thin asphalt surface, grubbed up like most well-pounded highways. For history's sake, a ribbon of bricks still remains for two-fifths of a mile at the start–finish line. Each time a driver howls across it, his teeth joggle a bit. Tangent

7

to the rectangle rise eighteen stands of varying size, haphazardly spaced around the track, providing permanent seating for two hundred and forty thousand spectators. Over on turn two huddles a posh thirty-two-unit VIP building, where suites rent for ten to twenty thousand dollars. The waiting list for one is years long. Against the inner rim of the main straightaway are the repair and refueling pits, like one-car service stations. Grafted onto one part of the infield is Gasoline Alley, a tightly policed area where two rows of serried garages hump into the air. Catercornered to the second turn hunches a statuesque museum, spanking clean and brimming with ancient race cars, trophies, memorabilia. A driver might lose control in the curve, blister through the fence, and smash his way into history.

In this setting, on May 30, at eleven in the morning, thirty-three cars will thunder five hundred miles in chase of a million dollars. That's more than double the money paid out by any other motor race. The man who straggles home last, maybe failing to complete even a single lap, will get fifteen thousand dollars. The winner will pocket over a quarter of a million dollars, given out after three hours of wrenching driving. On top of this, the winner can rake in an estimated million-dollar bonanza from product endorsements and personal appearances. An Indianapolis champion can book a speaking engagement every day of the year if he's up to it. Two-time winner Al Unser was, and his wife divorced him; she never got to see him any more.

Fifty million people or thereabouts go to auto races every year in this country, making the sport the second-biggest spectator draw, behind only horse racing (which has the advantage of pari-mutuel betting), and the Indianapolis 500 is racing's mother church. For the big day, a crowd of three hundred and fifty thousand people is expected, more than double the crowd that watches the Kentucky Derby, more than three times as many fans as throng to the Super Bowl, more people than mass

8

together for any single event of any kind in American spectating.

When drivers are just starting to race, showing no promise at all, they already picture themselves at Indianapolis, roaring down the straightaways. Drivers come to the track with speed in their heads, bankrolled mostly by car owners armed with corporation money, and the vision of their car flashing to victory. The odds say they will go back wherever they came from without getting in a lap of competition. It doesn't seem to matter. Neither the oldest race nor the longest, the 500 has come to be known as the greatest of them all. Affinities between the drivers and the race run deep.

"Sure there are other races. There is only one 500."

"For a driver to ever truly reach the heights of his profession, he must have the 500 as one of his credits. He can win everywhere else, but people will wonder what is wrong until he wins here. Once he does, the rest of his record won't mean a damn."

"Heaven for a race driver begins at the entrance to the Indianapolis Speedway. It ends at the exit."

"How often do you race for a million dollars?"

"When I first got into racing, I was taught right away that the race to shoot for was Indianapolis. I was told Indianapolis would change a man."

"Winning this race opens a lot of doors."

"The glory is so thick here you can touch it."

"The winner of the Indianapolis 500 is king of the mountain."

"It is assumed that everyone wants to win this race. Anyone who says different is either a liar or a fool."

There was Frank Lockhart. Slow-minded but doggedly determined, Lockhart would usually throw up when he was about to climb into a racing car. He wore the messiest uniforms around. A near illiterate, he never managed to learn to spell. Go play with the other kids, his mother would insist as he grew up. Instead, he would take things apart and put them back together again. He had little

9

time for anything else, marrying the only girl he ever dated. He could steer a race car as few men could, winning almost everywhere he went, setting tons of speed records. He wanted Indianapolis most of all. His mother had no money, living by sewing. He was broke. Desperation overtook reason. He mortgaged all the furniture in his mother's house to purchase tires to race at Indianapolis. He won in 1926.

There was Eddie Sachs. He started off by scrubbing dishes in the garage-area cafeteria, prowling for someone who would allow him to zoom a car. For a long while, no one would. Finally, he got behind the wheel and became a legend. He was the funniest man in racing; once he even brought a jazz band to the track to play for the crowd. He had the biggest mouth in racing. Announcers interviewing him after a victory could never get him to shut up; he once blabbed for an hour, and when he looked up, nearly everyone had gone home. He talked to himself a bit longer, then packed up and went. No one wanted to win the Indianapolis 500 more than Eddie Sachs. A glaze would appear in his eyes at the mention of the word "Indianapolis." Before the start of the race, as the bands played "Back Home Again in Indiana," he would sit slumped in his racer, tears streaming down his face. He came in second one year, losing by eight seconds. He finished third a year later, cursing his luck. He would say, "I think of the 500 every day of the year, every hour of the day, and when I sleep, too. Everything I've ever wanted in life is right here." Sachs swore that once he won the race he would give up the cars and talk the rest of his life. Nobody would ever know. He was killed in a fiery crash at Indianapolis in 1964.

Thousand-dollar entry fees in behalf of seventy-one race cars poured into the Speedway office for the Indianapolis 500 of 1976. To determine which thirty-three cars would take part in the race, all entries would be permitted to make qualifying attempts over the four weekend days preceding the weekend of the race. For ten miles, every car would be timed in hundredths of seconds, and the thirty-three fastest would be the field for the race.

The owners of the entries, for the most part, are very rich. Their hometowns are scattered across the country, and their occupations are scattered across the yellow pages. An oil man. A lumber man. A tire dealer. A frozen-juice entrepreneur. A playing-card manufacturer. A garbage magnate. An insurance man. A metal fabricator. Full-time race-car builders. Real-estate people. A thousand dollars also came from the president of Trans-Ocean Steamship Agency Incorporated, 29 Broadway, New York —from a man named Tassi Vatis. Vatis's fortune derives from ships, but his heart is in race cars. It is not entirely impossible—just close to it—that Tassi Vatis could place a young man like Johnny Parsons in his car and expect to win the Indianapolis 500.

In 1969, when he was doing pretty well in sprint cars and midgets—the lower forms of auto racing—Parsons was beginning to feel more and more that if his skills were really as good as he thought they were, he should enter that race in Indianapolis. It shouldn't be hard to do; he lived five miles away. But Parsons had more hope than ability. He came to the Speedway and was told by track officials to go back to the small ovals and learn more about race driving. Four more years passed before someone was willing to put him in an Indianapolis car and tell him to get it into the 500. He passed his rookie test, but he could not work his car up to the speed needed to make the starting lineup. Then, in 1974, Tassi Vatis was told of an up and coming driver named Johnny Parsons. He could really stand on the pedal. He was a future star, no question about it. Why not give him a shot in your Indianapolis car? Vatis, at this point, had been coming to Indianapolis for thirteen years without so much as a whiff of success. He had begun to think his time might never come. He had once said, "If I ever win this race, it will be like walking on water." The most successful of his cars had finished seventh in 1964. "All

11

right. All right," he said. "I'll try Parsons." On the final day of qualifications, with eight minutes left on the clock, Parsons whipped the Vatis car around the big oval and into the twenty-ninth starting slot, so far back he wouldn't be able to see the green flag. Being in the race, though, was enough to make him sway like a drunk. "I could hardly believe it. I danced a jig in my head. The greatest day of my life, it seemed. I was in the Indianapolis 500." He was in the race for eighteen laps, and then the car broke down. He was awarded twenty-sixth position. Parsons trudged home and listened to the finish of the race on the radio. Then in 1975, with a new Vatis car and more seasoning as a driver, Parsons began to glow. He qualified twelfth, surged to a strong fifth as late as the hundred and fortieth lap, when the transmission went on the car and he ended another race in the garage. He was paid nineteenth. "I've watched a lot of the drivers down the years, the really good ones and all, and in my experience it takes about two years at the Speedway before a man's ready to win," Vatis has said. "This year Johnny is ready. He can win the 500 this year, if it's to be us."

Parsons views the race as something of a mission. "It's difficult to explain what this race means to a racing driver. It's money, but it's also glory. There are a lot of people who drive race cars, and a lot of people who wish they could drive race cars. Not very many could put a car in this race. Of the thirty-three who will start, probably less than half have a real shot at coming up the winner. So anyone who is serious about driving racing cars has to think this race is the moon. Every driver has either considered or dreamed about coming here. I've dreamed and dreamed about it since I was a kid. One of the guiding points of my life is to win the Indianapolis 500."

★★★★★★★★★★★★★★★★

On the third day of practice, fourteen men are running their winged things around the tight ribbon of bricks and asphalt, seeking speed cautiously on the nasty, low-banked corners and long straightaways. Drivers and mechanics use the practice period to iron out problems with the car and to build confidence in their abilities. There is a ceaseless bellowing of snarling exhausts; the air is sharp with the peculiar acrid smell of heavy-duty racing oil.

The racers screaming past all bear commercial names. Alex Foods Special. Sugaripe Prune Special. Spirit of Indiana Special. Leader Card Racer. Scio Cabinet Special. Schlitz Special. Indianapolis is the meat market of professional auto racing, where expensive cars are the equal of moving billboards. Their flanks are covered by the decals of every company involved in their creation.

The big track is one of the hardest these drivers run on. Built for much slower-moving cars, it is narrow, just fifty feet wide in the straightaways and sixty feet wide in the turns. The bends are sloped at only nine degrees, twelve minutes. There's little room to regain control of a car after a spin. Some drivers hate the track and dread driving on it. Auto racing is the most dangerous sport in the world, and Indy cars are possibly the most frightening machines around. Every driver knows that unexpectedly, in a matter of minutes, he could be turned into a vegetable or snuffed out. The track has put fear in many drivers, and it has taken the lives of thirty-six. Driving the track is like playing music. You have to find a rhythm.

Fingering matter from his eyes, Bill Finley mutters, "Today maybe we'll find out if this son of a bitch'll run. Every new car is sick. That is my premise. We must take the car and find out what it needs to make it well and healthy. Some cars need more medicine than others."

Johnny Parsons booms out of the fourth turn and scrambles down the main straightaway, the car about three feet below the outside crash wall, the best position from which to approach the first corner. The car has four forward speeds that can get it up to top speed ("full bore") of around 205 miles per hour. In ten seconds. The cockpit is more cramped than a coffin. The seat is custom-molded to reduce fatigue. Five dials fill the panel facing Parsons, indicating lubricating-oil pressure, engine-waste temperature, engine revolutions per minute, lubricating-oil temperature, and turbocharger pressure. There's no speedometer; the closest thing to it is the dial for engine revolutions. Some teams stick a two-way radio in the driver's helmet to let the driver pass information to the crew while he's on the track, but it's hard to hear with the snorting of the cars. Parsons doesn't use one. Down the main straightaway, with the huge grandstands climbing over the course—inside and out—and flipping shadows over the pavement, Parsons feels as if he is "driving down a narrow hallway in a house and getting ready to make a sharp left turn into the bedroom."

A gate is ten feet from the first turn. Just before Parsons reaches it he steers the car to within six inches of the outside wall; then he twists the wheel less than an inch in the other direction, enough to bring the car gently downward. The throttle is about four inches deep, deeper than on most cars. "This is my security blanket. I like to know I have a lot of control over the car's speed." A quarter of the way into the turn, Parsons lifts up on the throttle around an inch for a fraction of a second. He lightly brushes the brakes. "Mainly to know they're there." There's no shifting of gears. He brings the car down till the inside tires creep about an inch onto the wide white stripe that runs around the inside of the track. Called the "line" or "groove," it is the quickest way around the Indianapolis Motor Speedway and following it involves entering and exiting the turns in as near a straight line as possible. This cuts the friction between tires and asphalt and doesn't require as much reduction in speed. You stay outside on the straightaways, inside on the turns, follow a straight line.

Top cornering speed is about 180. Parsons keeps his head back and looks halfway, four hundred feet, into the curve, so he gets a good feel for his trajectory. All the turns have the same radius and banking, but every one is different. Turn one feels narrow. By the time Parsons is halfway into the corner, he is back at full throttle. Steered mildly to the right, the car flows to the outside of the track and rockets out of the turn at full speed. Since the next straightaway is short, Parsons stays close to the wall—within a foot of it—throughout its length. Inside the cockpit, Parsons is constantly talking to himself, criticizing his performance. Too low in that corner. A bit close to the wall there. Keep it steady. Don't touch the brakes too much. That's a little low. Keep it high. He peppers himself with questions. Can I take that corner just a shade faster? How are the tires? Are they a little soft? Is the steering weak or strong? How's the oil pressure? Brakes? Is the car smooth? What's the engine temperature? Can't I get around any faster?

Parsons comes into turn two lower than he did the first turn, about two feet from the wall, because there's a slight hump (from the tunnel that burrows under the corner to allow traffic to enter the infield of the track). The hump is so slight that it's invisible to the naked eye, and you could crawl out on your hands and knees and not be able to find it. But to a racing driver blasting along, the hump feels like he's just run over a clock-radio. So acute is Parsons' sensitivity that he can feel if anything is loose on the car. He can tell if one of the tires is low on air, even a couple of pounds. "Tires are like the nerves on your fingers." He also has quite a nose. He can sniff if a bearing is about to burn out before it registers on the oil gauge.

No brakes before entering turns two and four, because the car's speed doesn't build up as much down the short straightaways. Parsons now ducks to the bottom of the second turn, letting up slightly on the throttle, and then drifts out near the wall. He relaxes his grip for the trip down the backstretch, the best place to check the gauges and look in the rearview mirrors to see if someone is overtaking you. Without any outer grandstands, the back straightaway seems about the width of a living room.

Tooling around the Indianapolis Speedway in a race car is nothing like ordinary motoring on the expressway. The basic idea is to go so wickedly fast that the car barely stays on the road and comes as close as possible to skating off into the wall without actually doing so. The man who gets around the fastest is the man who drives closest to the brink of disaster. You need an uncanny instinct for the exact play of a car at racing speed and in all kinds of racing situations. You have to know tricks like slipstreaming, which is a way to hitch a ride on a faster car. Getting right behind a car and into a low-pressure area creates a vacuum effect. This gives a tow to the trailing car, allowing it to run faster. Only thing is, the freeloader has to be within inches of the other car. All around the track, Parsons is being cooked by heat, dulled by fumes. The wind tears at him. The noise batters at him. He's on the lookout for birds. A bird can knock out a driver.

A superlative blend of eye-hand control is probably the trait that most separates an Indianapolis driver from drivers in lesser levels of the sport. Racers deal in inches and half inches. At 180 miles per hour, the car directly in front of a driver might spin out, and there is only a second perhaps to size up the situation and get out of it. The throttle jams wide open going into a turn. Perhaps a second and a half before the driver is stuffed in the wall. One of the basics of auto racing is to know when you're going to have an accident and accept it. The ordinary motorist, in emergencies, goes into a panic. In a crash that would send the motorist's blood pressure through the ceiling an Indy driver is all calm. Clobbering walls is part of his job.

"When an accident occurs, the first thing is to try to steer your way out of it," Parsons has said. "In a race, you try not to 'lock it up,' slam on the brakes, because this will flatten the tires and force a pit stop to have them changed. Lose you several laps. And once you lock it up, you're out of control. You can only go straight. You can't steer the car. You lock up a car only if there's no other choice. It makes sense to do it if you have to. If you hit another car with the wheels turning, you'll probably sail right over it. With the wheels locked, you're liable to smash into him and bounce off. A car out of control is unpredictable. Usually, when a car spins out in front of you, you aim right for it, because it won't be there by the time you get there."

Parsons is short and well-built, neither heavy nor thin. He has thick wrists and a thick neck. The result of years of exercise, isometrics, lifting weights, a hundred and fifty neck rolls every morning, they have been developed for one purpose—to absorb the stress of a racing car at speed. He has twenty-forty vision, which aviator glasses correct to twenty-twenty. Once he had his eyes tested for how fast they respond to stimuli and the results were unbelievably high. Race drivers have great vision. Have to. Nothing foggier than twenty-twenty corrected vision is allowed on the Speedway. Drivers are run through a tough physical of the sort jet fighter pilots must face.

17

Emphasis is on reflexes and depth perception. There are some drivers who would never pass an army physical who get on the track by learning to adapt to their handicaps. Three one-legged drivers have shown up, one of them managing a sixth place. But one-eyed drivers are out. No depth perception. Yet in the 1920s, when medical exams were more lax, a man named Tommy Milton came to the Speedway, and before he was through, he had two Indianapolis victories to his credit. Milton drove with his head cocked, and though he neither admitted nor denied it, the word was that he had vision in just one eye.

Pounding down the backstretch, Parsons is thinking of nothing but getting the car around as fast as possible. "Concentration is the key," he has said. "Every second that you don't concentrate completely you are losing time. We call concentration lapses 'brain fade.' When I'm out on the track, I forget people are watching me. Race drivers are only thinking of their cars. That has to be hammered into you, and you learn it best by hitting a lot of walls."

Off the racecourse, Parsons bangs around in a scruffy-looking 1970 Ford Econoline. Top speed is 100 miles per hour. Handling isn't so hot in the wind. Parsons hates being a passenger and does everything he can to avoid a trip in which he's not behind the wheel. He drives about ten miles over the speed limit. "You don't know what's going to happen on the highway. On the track, you drive offensively. Everyone's a pro there. On the highways, you drive defensively. You look out for nuts. I never feel scared on the racing track. I've had some real chills run up and down my spine on public roads."

Gripping the wheel harder, Parsons barrels into the third turn, the roughest on the course, where southerly winds can shove a car off the corner. You have to really fight the car in turn three. To cancel the breeze, Parsons works the car down beneath the white line onto the rough inside apron.

Courage plays a part in racing, though drivers differ in their boldness. There are so-called "strokers" or "coast and collectors" who know they have small chance of winning. They plug away, saving their engines, just hoping to finish the race and collect some money. Parsons has said, "I drive cars to the limit. As fast as they'll go. Finishing fourth or third is not worthwhile. I've done that. I want to win." Parsons drives cars into the ground. "Give me a race car that will go 200," he says, "and I'll drive it 200."

Parsons hugs the wall in the short chute between three and four. No brakes, a slight easing on the throttle, and he floats into the fourth corner. The smoothest of the four corners, a beautiful turn. Parsons wishes all the turns were the fourth turn. A lot of grandstands border the turn, making it, like the first corner, seem narrower that it is. Parsons feels as if he is leaving the bathroom and returning to the long hallway leading to the bedroom.

"Every day I'll try to go a little faster. You sneak up on speed. If you climbed into a car and went 185 without working up to it gradually, you'd probably get sick. You concentrate so hard you tire quickly. There are other races that are more physically draining than Indianapolis, but there are no other races as mentally draining. You're constantly alert for possible changes in the track or in the car. Every year the track is different. The weather alone changes the way it runs. I'm always checking my opposition. I make mental notes on every driver. A driver I trust I'll run within four inches of. If I don't trust someone, I'll stay two feet away. I'll never try to pass him in a corner. I'm always seeing how I can gain a few feet. You don't try ridiculous things, but you must be aggressive. The winner of the race must drive as fast as his car will let him. Not unsafely, but maybe a little past the point of safety."

A car whips by. Another. Another. Parsons growls

through the exit of the fourth turn, his foot nailed to the throttle, the engine up to full bore. He comes steaming down the main straightaway and whistles past the starting line. In the pits, a crewman hits a stopwatch with his thumb. It shows 50.9 seconds, a speed of 176.917 miles per hour. "He's got to go faster," the crewman says.

★★★★★★★★★★★★★★★★

The first man to take his rookie test is Bobby Olivero. Though slight and nearly chinless, he is an impressive driver. On any first attempt to enter the race, regardless of his experience on other tracks, a driver must weather a two-phase driving test. He must turn twenty laps (fifty miles) at an average speed of 160 miles per hour, without wavering more than 1 mile an hour below or 2 miles an hour above that speed. Then he completes twenty more laps at any comfortable speed of 165 or better. While he bowls around the course, several veteran drivers space themselves at the curves and study the rookie's behavior at speed. Is he smooth in the corners? Is he scared of the walls? Does traffic frighten him? Is he keeping a consistent groove? Afterward, they must unanimously confirm his skills if he is to be allowed to try to qualify for the big race.

Olivero does his laps. They consume roughly an hour. He looks smooth. His lap times are on target. Sitting on his jury are Dick Simon, Tom Sneva, Tom Bigelow, Bill Vukovich, Johnny Parsons. The drivers assemble in the chief steward's office to mull over the run. Olivero is brought in. A clipboard with sheets recording Olivero's lap speeds is handed around to the drivers. Silence in the room, some nervous clearing of throats. Olivero looks on quietly, anxiously. He feels he did well. He would sell more than his soul to make this race.

Parsons scoops up the clipboard. His eyes skitter down the speeds. He frowns, waggles his head. "Oh, I don't know," he says.

Sneva snatches the board. He knits his brow. "No. No," he says.

"Let me take a look at those," Vukovich says. Sneva hands him the clipboard. "Jesus. Oh, God, no."

Olivero, having felt pretty good when he came in, appears on the brink of a massive heart attack.

Bigelow and Simon gawk at the times, their faces impassive. They blink, as if to adjust to a sudden too-bright light. "Wow!" Bigelow murmurs. "Wow!"

No one says anything for a bit.

Parsons clears his throat. He speaks up. "Well, Bobby, if nobody else is going to say anything, all I can say is there's the race at Ontario coming up on Labor Day."

"How about Pocono?" Bigelow allows. "That's sooner."

"Nah," Parsons says. "I don't think that he'll even be ready for Pocono."

The color has drained from Olivero's face. He seems to be pondering the possibility that, at twenty-nine, he can still make a go of it in professional baseball.

Together, all the drivers explode into raucous laughter. They lift themselves up and pump Olivero's hand. He passed with ease.

A. J. Foyt marches out for a practice run. He comes strutting out of the garage area, walking almost on his toes, a blue racing cap slanted on his head. He seems to get huger and huger. His massive frame suggests a football player. His face juts as sharp as a hatchet. Foyt's hair is thinning noticeably, though his arms and shoulders are as powerful as ever.

"Hey A. J.," someone hollers. "Come here, A. J. Come on here."

"Let's go Foyt."

"Whoooooooe-wheet," comes a whistle.

"Go get 'em, A. J."

His face is deadly serious. His look seems almost menacing. Depending on how fast his car is running, he may throw a glance, the beginning of a smile, a small wave. Kids dart up for Foyt's autograph and others are just hanging around. One man comes up, he is about forty, and he says, "Gonna win, A. J.?"

"I didn't come here for a vacation," Foyt says.

Foyt clumps out to the pit area where his gleaming Coyote car, number 14, red as blood, is parked along the wall. His crew is buzzing around it, all in matching uniforms—the general atmosphere of big-time auto racing. No one has built a record quite like Foyt's. For years, he has been considered the fastest and most versatile driver alive. There is no accounting for the silver cups, trophies, medals, awards, and whatnot he has been given for his victories. He could probably melt them down and build a house of silver. Every year, his Indy cars run about ten other championship races at tracks sprawled around the country. Foyt has won fifty-four of these races, far more than any other driver. (Mario Andretti is second with thirty-two.) And Foyt has won in almost every other form of racing, too. He lives in Houston where, among other things, he owns an engine shop, a Chevrolet dealership, a six-hundred-and-forty-acre ranch where he raises cattle and horses, and part interest in a bank. He owns oil property in Louisiana, real estate, and some warehouses. Two years ago, he fell into horse racing; he has had eight victories with his stable and hopes to put a horse in the Kentucky Derby. "I like 'em as much as the cars if they win. If they don't win, it's the same thing, the sons of bitches are no good."

Foyt is a millionaire several times over. He is the king, and all the other drivers—whether they like him or not—have immense respect for his skill on the racetrack. When

Foyt was a three-year-old, his father, now a mechanic on the car, gave him a gas-powered miniature racer. At six, he began driving it at 50 miles per hour. Starting at eighteen, every May for five years he scraped together money and went to watch the Indianapolis race. He qualified in 1958 at the age of twenty-three. He won on his fourth try. "Hoping never done a thing," Foyt has said. "It's wanting that does it. I've wanted to do things. If you want to win bad enough, you win." Now forty-one, Foyt has been driving for twenty-nine years and has reached the point where most of his friends, his father, and his wife hope he will retire. But he won't because he hasn't won the Indianapolis 500 a fourth time, which would be a record, and he intends to keep on racing until he does.

For sheer crowd appeal, no other driver even comes close to Foyt. He has magnetized a huge contingent of fans. He is to his sport what Babe Ruth and Joe Namath and Arnold Palmer have been to theirs. He might as well be given Indianapolis. Instances. He has won the race more times than any other active driver (three). He has driven more miles at the track than anyone else racing (6,402.5). He's been the fastest qualifier more times (four). He's led more laps (477). He's won more money here (over eight hundred thousand dollars). Foyt owns his own car and is his own chief mechanic. His sponsor is a Kalamazoo, Michigan, businessman by the name of Jim Gilmore. Gilmore is a good-looking man with a joyful expression. He owns radio and television stations, Holiday Inns, an advertising agency, and a car dealership.

Foyt drops himself into his car, the engine churns to life—its roar like the thunder of a freight train—and he rolls onto the track. He rockets around the oval at a speed of 188.6 miles per hour, the fastest anyone has gone.

Johnny Rutherford has been moving fast, too—187, 188 miles per hour. As obliging as Foyt is irascible, Rutherford steamed into the limelight in 1974, when he started from near the back of the pack, surged quickly to the front, and outlasted Foyt to win his first Indian-apolis 500. He dedicated the victory to his father, who was dying of cancer. Last year, he sopped home second when rain shortened the race, and he maintains that if the skies had not opened when they did, he would have won again. His motive this year is revenge. "I'd like to win at least three more times," he says. Thirty-eight years old and a spare, mild-appearing man of pebbly chatter from Fort Worth, Texas, Rutherford grew up gluing together plastic models of race cars and painting pictures of them. Finally, he got into what he painted, struggling in the jalopies, sliding the dusty dirt tracks on the county-fair circuit. He showed early promise, but his career was stalled frequently by serious accidents. In a wild flip over the guardrail at an Ohio track, he broke both his arms. Many thought Rutherford's career was over. For four or five years, it looked like it was. He burned his hands badly in another crash. Then he came back. "When you're hurt so badly and you see so many others killed in this sport, there are times when you think of quitting. But I say to myself, 'What the hell else could I do?' " Rutherford looks on auto racing as an art form. "All you have to do is look at a slow-motion film of cars together on a racetrack. It's just like a ballet."

For a while now, Rutherford has been in a position to pick the cars he will drive. Any owner who gets him is lucky. His car this year is owned by McLaren Racing, a race car company formed by Bruce McLaren, a superior driver who was killed at the wheel. Hy-Gain, the CB-radio people, have also plowed money into the car, prodding Rutherford to crow a lot about CB radios. When he arrived this year, Rutherford began to say that he sensed the same feeling he did two years ago, that if he takes things slowly and pays attention to details, he will take the whole boodle. With Foyt and Rutherford flaunting so much early speed, the word around the track is that the Texans have come to Indianapolis loaded for bear.

Up and down the pit apron, serious-looking crewmen slouch with stopwatches and speed charts cradled in their hands, shaking their heads in wonder. What's he running? How did Foyt do? What'd you catch him in? The charts equate time with miles per hour. For example, 45.21 seconds is 199.071; that's the track record. Fifty seconds is 180.000. Gossip in the pits is that it will take at least that to make the race.

Time more than anything else is what defines how good an Indy car is and, day by day, whether it is doing the job. The margin between a winner and a borderline car is measured and recorded in brief, merciless wipes of a stopwatch hand. For instance, the separation between the man favored to take the race and a dark-horse candidate is likely to average around three miles per hour. Three miles an hour around the Indianapolis Motor Speedway works out to two-fifths of a second. For the middling driver, sweating it out just to make the field, the difference between what he is running and the times of the slowest qualifiers is often less than a tenth of a second a lap. These differences are hellishly difficult to reduce. Lap after lap will be turned, still a tenth too slow. Mechanics scratch down every change they make on a car and how much time it shaves off a lap till they come up with the blend that shakes out the most speed. Part of the game at Indianapolis is to hide your speed from the competition, so as to lull them into complacency rather than frighten them into improving their equipment. This is done best by "sandbagging." A driver will purposely back off on specific portions of the track, normally the turns, so that other teams will clock him slower than he's running. The sandbagging team sends out four timers, one per corner, and for four laps the driver will slow down on a different corner. By taking the fastest time on each turn, the team will know how fast its car is running.

"Can't believe it," a sharp-faced crewman says, consulting his watch. "Only 51.3. How ya figure that? He must have stopped out there."

"Probably doing some grocery shopping," allows a slightly stooped man.

"Hell, I'd eat a bucket of it if we could go faster."

"I'll tell you, we don't run this race on no track. We run it on a stopwatch."

★★★★★★★★★★★★★★★★

On this same rectangle where race drivers are trying to squeeze speed out of winged machines, cattle and sheep a century ago were moving along slowly and a fertile innovator was dreaming the whole thing up. The man's name was Carl Fisher. He was something of a genius at that indispensable American strategy: publicity. Having lost what interest he had in subjects like long division, Fisher dropped out of school at the age of twelve and went to work as a news butcher, hawking newspapers and candies on the railroad cars. Business boomed. This was 1886. As his boyhood went by, Fisher worked in a grocery, in a bank, in a book store; he ran a bicycle repair shop and he opened up a bicycle store. Always he longed for a bigger world than his surroundings provided. When the first automobile came to Indianapolis, it was Carl Fisher who bought it, and in 1900, he started his own car agency, selling Oldsmobiles. Promote, promote, promote, he kept telling himself. Acquiring a big Winton, he worked the county fairs. Put up five hundred dollars and I'll race a horse, any horse, he would tell whoever would listen. Saddle up the quickest four legs in the world, and we'll go any distance you like. Actually, Fisher insisted the distance exceed two hundred yards.

He was no fool. As the races unfolded, the horse would pour ahead on early acceleration, would put together a handy lead, and then lose miserably in the final few lengths. Grinning sheepishly, Fisher would pocket his winnings and take off for the next fair, where history would repeat itself. When Fisher was about to introduce a new Stoddard-Dayton, he arranged to have the car lashed to a gigantic balloon. He lowered himself behind the wheel, and for several hours he hung over Indianapolis at two thousand feet. It became evident that Fisher was one of those thinkers who could push back the boundaries of the mind. In 1904, he organized the Prest-O-Lite Company, its product being the first gas supply tank for automobile headlights. Prest-O-Lite made Fisher a millionaire.

When he was not contemplating the moon, Fisher was screaming around in racing cars, and in 1905, he was part of the American racing team for the James Gordon Bennett Cup races in Europe, a coveted competition of the day. The German, English, Italian, and French cars all blew off the Americans. "Why are our cars such lemons?" Fisher wondered. An idea flew in. He sketched out in his head a laboratory, a tremendous rectangular proving ground. There all manner of inventions, innovations, and developments could be assayed for use in ordinary passenger cars. Why not build the thing himself? Why not conduct auto races on the side? Why not use the admission money from the races to keep the place going? Fisher thought he would build a speed course that conceivably could concern the world.

At the time this idea planted itself in Carl Fisher's head, Americans had already been watching motor races regularly for most of ten years, usually on dirt horse tracks, or on prefabricated board courses—racetracks to go—or else right out on the open road. He had reason to think people would pay to watch men cheat death in flat-out contests of speed.

29

Carl Fisher inspired confidence. He said he was going to build a flying bathtub, and you thought about where you wanted to go in it. Before too long, he had talked three other pioneer manufacturers of motor cars in Indianapolis into believing in his big proving ground to the extent that they would help build it. In the autumn of 1908, the foursome—Fisher, Arthur Newby, James Allison, and Frank Wheeler—got together seventy-two thousand dollars and bought three hundred and twenty acres of farmland northwest of town. The land abutted a highway and a railroad. Four hundred and fifty men and three hundred mules began the laborious process of laying down a course of gravel, crushed limestone, stone dust, and liquefied tar. There was no precedent to go on. Nobody had ever built such a private speed course before, not anywhere in the world—and wouldn't for some time to come. If it worked, it worked.

The maiden race was to run on June 5, 1909. Not long before, Henry Ford had unveiled his "universal" car, the Model T, with a price tag of eight hundred and fifty dollars. On another side of the world, explorers Robert Peary and Matthew Henson, with some help from four Eskimos, had come across the North Pole. The Indianapolis race turned out to be a balloon race, since the track surface was still unfinished. Fisher himself was a contestant in the race. He tossed out hundreds of red roses as he sailed toward heaven and floated somewhere into Tennessee.

Two months later, mule teams poured the last of the tar, and unable to contain his impatience any longer, Fisher sent the automobiles running. The track fell apart. It was unable to withstand the pummeling from the hard tires. Now the track was here, now it wasn't. Stones shot through the air like bullets. With each event, conditions worsened. More cracks. More potholes. Less track. In the main event, a driver and "mechanician" were killed, the first Indianapolis deaths. In a subsequent race, Charles

Metz lost control, screamed off the course, scaled an embankment, soared through the air for a hundred feet, careened into the crowd, and killed two spectators and his mechanic. The race was called off early, and the track was repaved with bricks. Brick upon brick, three million two hundred thousand bricks were slapped down in sixty-three days, conceivably a bricklaying record. On December 17, 1909, a ceremonial "gold" brick (actually bronze and brass, a carburetor-body alloy, fifty-two pounds) was laid to dedicate "the world's greatest speedway." Following the dedication, the brick was removed for display in the Speedway office. Someone made off with it when the office was shut down during World War II. The Speedway is still looking for it.

James J. Jeffries, one-time heavyweight champion of the world, got to take the first lap on the new surface. He liked the ride. Racing was tried right away. Five hundred paying customers showed up and turned into icicles. It was nine degrees out. When the thermometer picked up, Fisher ran motorcycle races. He ran stock car races. He ran altitude tests. He ran airplane races. He ran a race between an airplane and a peculiar propeller-driven car; the plane won. He put on another balloon race. He put on a Memorial Day program of forty-two short races. He put on everything but an ostrich race, and he considered that. He finally couldn't think of anything else to put on. Thereafter, he declared, there would be a single race a year, and it would be the longest race the public could possibly stand. Thought was given to a twenty-four-hour race. People would fall asleep, it was reasoned. A thousand-mile race? People might not nod off, but they would be drowsy. Fisher settled on five hundred miles, to be run every Memorial Day.

They called it the Indianapolis 500 when the first race was run in 1911. Three thousand wooden hitching posts were set up for the carriage trade. To get in you paid fifty cents, a dollar, or a dollar fifty. Ladies arrived in

31

long, fluttering dresses and carrying parasols. Men came in floppy cloth caps and straw hats. Children came in diapers. Forty cars—stubby, unstable contraptions that resembled cardboard boxes on wheels—qualified for the race. Ralph DePalma, a front-running driver of the time, counseled contestants in a prerace interview on the evils of wayward tastes. In his words: "Many of the biggest automobile races in the history of the sport have been lost the night before." He offered no details. Ray Harroun, a clean-liver, took six hours and forty-two minutes of strenuous driving to win the race as an admiring crowd of eighty thousand cheered him on. An engineer for Marmon who had come out of retirement for the event, Harroun believed in being his own man. Everyone carried a riding mechanic, who would pump oil, change tires, and alert the driver when he was about to be run over by a faster machine. Harroun preferred his own company, so he got an eight-by-three-inch mirror and welded it to the car with iron bars, creating the first rearview mirror. As it happened, the mirror vibrated so much at speed that Harroun couldn't see a thing out of it.

The race was exciting enough. At one point, the car of Arthur Greiner shed a tire. Yawing crazily down the track, the racer propelled Greiner and his mechanic into orbit. The mechanic was tossed against a fence and instantly killed. Greiner landed on a cushion of grass and suffered a broken arm. Unmindful of any injuries, spectators swarmed across the infield and pressed close to the bodies; soldiers had to beat them back to clear space for doctors. Another driver lost control as he barreled down the main straightaway. His mechanic, figuring trouble lay ahead, leapt out. He tripped and fell, and was mowed down by the car he had just been sitting in. He suffered a broken leg. A woman in a box seat worked herself up to a point of frenzy, passed out, and tumbled from her chair, nearly inciting a riot from the people she landed on. She was heavy.

Harroun won by a full lap, averaging 74.6 miles an hour. He went home with ten thousand dollars from a purse of twenty-five thousand. He also retired again.

Next year, up went the winning speed by four miles an hour and up went the winning purse by fifteen thousand. Joe Dawson was the winner, but the real story of the race was Ralph DePalma. He led the event effortlessly for much of the going. With less than three laps left, he was ten miles ahead. Then he had a tough break. His car stopped. Displaying bitter determination, he and his mechanic hopped out and began shoving the car around the course. Vicariously, the crowd tried to add some shoves of its own. They got it through another two miles before they pooped out. DePalma walked in eleventh and was paid three hundred and eighty dollars. Happily, he made it to Victory Lane (driving) three years later.

By the third running of the race, the Europeans were interested. The American press became aroused. *Motor Age* said boldly: "On the rim of a colossal brick saucer are perched the mute cars of four nations, foreboding monsters that sound a menacing challenge when gasoline and oil course through their hardened veins. In the chaotic camps, where grimy men sweat and toil under the lash of Ambition, the champions of four nations are waiting to put the strength, stamina, and strategy of America to the crucial test." It didn't ruffle the foreigners. Jules Goux, driving a Peugeot, took the money back to France with him. As he sped to victory, he knocked back four bottles of vintage champagne during his pit stops (it was hot out), one of the few times the driver ran on alcohol.

The Speedway had only been a going concern for several years when it became plain that its destiny was as a racetrack rather than as a proving ground. Breakthroughs continued to be worried out in far-flung laboratories by forgetful men in long white coats, and car makers began to build their own elaborate test areas, better suited to their purposes. Anyway, as the years wore on, Carl Fisher began to lose interest in the Speed-way. He now trained his imagination on developing some resort property he had gotten hold of. Fisher had bought a winter home down south sight unseen, another of those rainbows that wicketed his horizons. He went down before the 1913 race to look it over, and before returning, he acquired a sizable swatch of land for what seemed a cheap fifty thousand dollars. It wasn't so cheap. The land was in a mangrove swamp on a long peninsula. If inclined to get there, which no one seemed to be, you swam or went by boat. Fisher, however, saw beyond alligators and smelly water. Perhaps if a bridge to the mainland were built, perhaps if some other improvements were made, a great city might be carved out of a strip of jungle. A winter dreamland. People sunning themselves on the sand. Golf courses. Polo fields. Casinos. Girlie shows. Orange juice. That, at least, was the landscape in Fisher's mind. Everyone else saw mud. Over the ensuing few years, Fisher brought in a workload of machinery, men, and two elephants; he cleared the jungle, filled in the swamp, created small residential islands. The city Fisher was building had no name as yet. Years down the road, people would call it Miami Beach.

Events of another sort occupied the mind of Eddie Rickenbacker. Rickenbacker was attempting to sell the world cars with four-wheel brakes. The world wasn't buying. "Why not rubber-band engines while you're at it?" Consequently, the Rickenbacker Motor Company went bust, a year after Rickenbacker stepped aside. Although badly in debt, he had a friend willing to put up the money to get him back on his feet. Rickenbacker looked around and became drawn to the Allison Engineering Company, which, among other things, thumbed out bearings for aircraft engines and gears for navy dirigibles. These looked like sound products. Rickenbacker went to see James Allison, at the time in partial retirement. "I want to buy your company," he said. "Don't buy my company," Allison replied. "I like to have a desk to put my feet on. Go buy the Indianapolis Motor Speedway."

Rickenbacker knew something about racetracks. In the years leading up to World War I, he had been one of the best racing drivers around. He drove relief in the first Indianapolis 500 and finished sixth in the 1916 race. In his youth, almost everything he did nearly killed him. Between the ages of three and ten, he ran head-on into a horse-drawn streetcar, fell into a cistern, tumbled out of a tree, and got his foot stuck in a train track as an engine barreled down on him. As a military aviator during the war, Rickenbacker, of course, was a legend, doing in twenty-two German bombers and four observation balloons. He took great pride in turning the tables on seemingly hopeless odds. The deal to buy the track was consummated in August 1927: one used racetrack for cash and bonds totaling seven hundred thousand dollars.

Meanwhile, Fisher's dream of Miami Beach was bursting into reality. A couple would come down and bang, another lot gone. Up went casinos, restaurants. In came the money. During one of his routines, Will Rogers cracked of Fisher: "He rehearsed the mosquitoes until they wouldn't bite until after you bought." Fisher still wasn't satisfied, as any dreamer wouldn't be. The fortune he assembled from Miami he poured into the development of Montauk Point, the furthest tip of Long Island, in the hopes of fashioning yet another Miami Beach. This time, luck ran against him. The boom period abruptly ended, and Fisher lost nearly all he had—some five million dollars—in Montauk. Frank Wheeler, despondent over a diabetic condition, had shot himself in 1921. James Allison died of pneumonia during the summer of 1928. Arthur Newby, following a lengthy illness, died in the fall of 1933. In 1939, Fisher, finally broken of health and spirit, died of a gastric hemorrhage while in a Florida hospital.

He died a comparatively poor man. The year of his death, Miami Beach was assessed for municipal tax purposes at more than sixty-one million dollars.

The first thing Rickenbacker did was build a golf course on the infield of the track. He also paved the entire course with asphalt, skipping a small portion at the starting line. The race was turning wickedly cruel. Five men died in 1933. Two more went in 1934. Four went in 1935. Some cars seemed built by the Devil himself. They would kill, then next year return and kill again. A mechanic named Louis Meyer arrived from California and swept to victory in 1928, 1933, and 1936, the first man to win the race three times. In 1937, running second, Meyer clouted the second-turn wall, decided it was time he found a safer way to feed himself, and started building racing engines.

When World War II came, Rickenbacker shut down the track, and over the war years, the Speedway wallowed in the decay of neglect. By the time peace was declared, the ancient wooden grandstands looked as if they would collapse as soon as the first ticket holder got comfortable. The bricks on the track were speckled with cracks. Grass grew up between them. The infield was steeped in weeds that climbed past the shoulders. People who saw the track thought it looked like a wilderness. Rickenbacker gathered in the situation with a sour disposition. The Speedway had never been that close to his heart, he had spent relatively little of his time involved with it, and he saw no reason to drain his wallet any further. He doubted whether anyone cared whether the place got running again. Already he was envisioning the acreage dotted by one- and two-story homes, a supermarket, a school, a gas station, a nice restaurant. Anyway, in 1938, he had bought Eastern Airlines, a peanut carrier with a mismatched assortment of planes, and he was concerned with beefing up its lackluster business. Money, as he saw it, was up in the air.

Wilbur Shaw, however, could not accept the thought

of the big speed course going under, one reason being that he had made so much money there. Shaw had won the 500 three times—in 1937, 1939, and 1940. He was a charger. In 1931 he sailed his car over the northeast wall, got out as if it were what he had planned to do, and hopped into another racer. Shaw shopped around and got Rickenbacker together with a Terre Haute capitalist who was loaded. His name was Anton Hulman, Jr. He had attended more than a dozen races. He would say, "A lot of times I used to sit at home and watch the people flash by on the Old National Road, a dirt road then, that ran between Terre Haute and Indianapolis. I'd see a lot more strange automobiles than I'd usually see. Foreign makes and all. It was as if word had come from above that the world was coming to an end, and everyone was trying to escape. It struck me that this Indianapolis was something that was worth preserving. Suddenly, it looked like it was up to me to do it."

Hulman had had a lifetime accented by sports. His father, who owned a general wholesale firm in Terre Haute, was a state champion bicyclist. Hulman pumped a good bike himself. His father also owned an old Pierce-Arrow, which Hulman would borrow to fetch fresh eggs. On some of these trips, he would meet up with a Stutz Bearcat or some similar four-wheeled threat. Engines revved, gear shifts were grabbed. Vroom. Driving like the wind, Hulman scored more than his share of victories. He was at his best, though, on foot. At prep school (Lawrenceville, three years; Worcester Academy, one year), Hulman was a pole vaulter, a broad jumper, a shot-putter, a high jumper, and a hurdler. He competed in intramural baseball, intramural basketball, and varsity football. He entered Yale in 1920. He won seven letters. Altogether, Hulman won nearly a hundred medals at prep school and college.

He could also run a business empire. When Hulman took over his father's general wholesale firm, Hulman and Company, it produced thousands of items, but only one in real quantity. This was Clabber Girl Baking Powder. But one hot number didn't seem like much to Hulman, no matter how well it moved. Everybody in the country might be buying it, but everybody could stop buying it. In succeeding years, he displayed a head for knowing what people wanted. As product after new product was added to the shelves, Hulman went on a buying spree, swallowing up gas companies, breweries, refineries, real estate, a chemical company, newspapers, part of a railroad, a Coca-Cola bottling plant, and on and on. Hulman parlayed a tidy family fortune into something that would nicely see an emerging nation through its formative years.

By the oddest of ironies, Hulman had in his youth gone south with his father and Carl Fisher to look over investment possibilities in Miami Beach. The senior Hulman wasn't interested; he frankly didn't think Miami would fly. Years later, however, his son was one of the few men alive who had money and was willing to put it into Indianapolis, which looked to be one of the worst investments to come along. Hulman agreed to buy the track for seven hundred and fifty thousand dollars, just fifty thousand more than Rickenbacker had paid twenty years earlier. The deal was closed in November 1945. Seemingly as an afterthought, Hulman announced he was not buying the place to make money.

Hulman tackled in earnest the problem of revitalizing the Speedway. Facilities were replaced and new ones added. The whole place was given a coat of paint, putting it in splendid fettle. Hulman named Wilbur Shaw as general manager of the Speedway. He announced the running of the Indianapolis 500 for May of 1946. Soon thereafter, a mechanic announced he was grooming a Mercedes-Benz, acquired secondhand, to run in the race—its first owner had been Adolf Hitler. George Robson won the race, as a hundred and seventy-five thousand people swarmed through the gates. Speedway personnel didn't know what to do. Lined up outside was possibly the longest traffic jam in the history of the world. Thousands of people were still in line to get in when the checkered flag flew for Robson. They had seen nothing but the backs of people's cars. They had seen no car numbers, only license plates. Somewhat more attention to traffic movement would be paid next year.

The next important date in Speedway history was 1948, when Mauri Rose scored his third victory (to go with wins in 1941 and 1947), thus elevating him to the select company of Louis Meyer and Wilbur Shaw. Rose was a short and skinny man, moody and outspoken, with a brush haircut and a square moustache. He was a bit of a braggart; the first thing he would tell a new acquaintance was how stupendous a driver he was. "You think you're good," he might say. "Myself, I'm great."

The making of the next Indianapolis legend had its origins in 1961, when the indomitable A. J. Foyt fought off a persistent Eddie Sachs in a stirring duel to win his first 500. He, of course, wasn't finished. He went on to take the race twice more—in 1964 and 1967—along with every other motor contest in existence. History is waiting for the first four-time winner. Louis Meyer is retired and lives on a farm in Indianapolis. Mauri Rose is retired and lives in Warren, Michigan. Wilbur Shaw was killed in an inexplicable plane crash into a corn field in 1954. Foyt races against ghosts.

Today, Tony Hulman is in his mid-seventies. He still serves as president and guiding spirit of the Speedway, about which he feels like a mother toward her first-born. He is a handsome man, with a full head of slate-gray hair and a solid jaw. His face is lined in the right places. Hulman is a man of massive, somewhat grim dignity, with a warm, disarming smile. Sitting in his office one day, sipping coffee out of a Styrofoam cup, he said, "The Speedway today is as much a civic enterprise as a private enterprise. That, I think, has something to do with its success. Folks around here believe that they own it, not me. It's like the United States. Everyone who lives here kind of figures he owns a chunk of it. I can't imagine the race ever not being run. I guess I can envision, years and years down the road, people getting about in rockets or something, riding light rays maybe, but they'll still be showing up and watching the cars go five hundred miles."

Hulman is a millionaire several times over, although Hulman and Company, which got the dollars flowing, is less than a shadow of its former self, as is the entire general wholesale business. Making money with the 500 is no longer easy either. Hulman wishes to keep the race big and to preserve its traditional majesty, and he refuses to streamline in order to cut down expenses. As a result, its costs tend to exceed its revenues. Hulman makes up the difference.

Despite his preoccupation with race cars, Hulman himself was never really inclined to drive. Only once did he take a whirl around the track in a racing machine. Wilbur Shaw was driving, and Hulman was wedged in beside him, barely able to move. This was 1950. "Take it easy, will you, Wilbur," Hulman advised as they started off. "Just take it easy." Shaw floored the accelerator and rocketed down the homestretch. As they approached the first turn, which is of ample width for one race car to get around, particularly when there are no others on the track, Hulman was positive there was no room. At the 120 miles per hour or so that Shaw was driving, the curve looked to Hulman like the eye of a needle, like an alleyway. "Slow down, Wilbur, slow down," Hulman yelled. Shaw barreled around the turn and got the car up to full bore again down the backstretch. As they blasted along, Hulman kept walloping Shaw. "Slow down, Wilbur. Slow down." Hulman's nails were bitten far back. At one point, he knocked Shaw's foot off the accelerator. Shaw put it back on. "You're going to kill both of us," Hulman hollered. He began to imagine the nature of his funeral and ran through the guest list. After two laps, Shaw finally relented and let Hulman out. Hulman's knees were shaking. He never again wanted to take a lap in a race car around the Speedway. It was no fun at all.

Johnny Parsons is standing around in the pit area waiting for his car to arrive. A hot, muggy day. The air is so dry your sweat evaporates almost instantaneously. Cars swarm by like flies on the pavement. The crew rolls the Ayr-Way WIRE Special out of the alley, pausing to have the tire pressure checked by Goodyear technicians, and then continues on through a gate pulled open by track security men and onto the concrete surface of the pits. The crew wastes little time setting up, while Parsons gets himself ready. He has on a beige fire-resistant Nomex driving suit speckled with patches: Goodyear, Valvoline, Bell, Champion, Ayr-Way, WIRE, the City of Speedway. His underwear and shoes are of Nomex. He stuffs wax earplugs into his ears, kneading the wax with his fingers; to sit head pressed against the engine would leave a driver partially deaf. He yanks on a head sock and then ties a red and white bandana, like a bank robber, around his mouth. He tugs on his helmet, which is similar to a jet pilot's: expensive, solid, tight-fitting. The helmet is white with red and blue streaks, and stitched to it is an apron that Parsons tucks into his suit to protect his neck. He pulls down a visor, then slips on a pair of Nomex gloves that resemble gardener's gloves. Looking like he's ready to blast off for Pluto, he squirms into the winged machine and fastens a seat belt and two shoulder harnesses around his body. A crewman pokes an aircraft-type inertia starter into the rear of the engine; the cars have no starters of their own. The engine catches with a wail and Parsons spurts onto the track.

Johnny Parsons learned about race cars early.

Born in 1944, in Newhall, California, he was given the name John Wayne Parsons, a decision his parents reached after seeing a John Wayne movie. With the same first name but spelling it Johnnie, his father was also a racing driver and sporadically a sheet metal worker, pursuing both careers to raise a family. The marriage broke up when young Johnny turned six. His mother moved to Indianapolis, where she married Duane Carter, another racing driver. Parsons and his sister (two years older) moved in with their aunt briefly and then went to live with their grandmother. Winning in the midgets and the sprints, his father had begun to piece together a respectable career of his own in the race world. He got into Indianapolis cars. At best, young Parsons had a hazy notion of what it was his father did. He got paid to drive absurd-looking cars very fast, he knew, but that was about it. Every race seemed the same. Listening to the radio in his grandmother's house on May 30, 1950, Parsons felt "pretty good, I guess. Neat, I suppose. I know my grandmother went absolutely wild." His father had just won the Indianapolis 500.

His father became famous, running around giving speeches and pushing products. Meanwhile, Parsons settled in with his mother and her new family. There were two half-brothers, "Pancho" (now racing against Parsons at Indianapolis) and Dana (working on a racing career of his own). In 1953, Parsons got his first look at the Indianapolis Motor Speedway, where both his father and stepfather were driving. He thought it a fairyland. Over the long, slow weeks of practice, he would race his bicycle around the open field beside the track. His com-

43

petition included Bill Vukovich and Gary Bettenhausen, two sons of drivers themselves. Both of their fathers eventually died at Indianapolis. They themselves would come to race there. In their fertile imaginations, the dusty field was the big Speedway and the two-wheelers were powerful racing machines bowling around the asphalt and bricks. Parsons did poorly in these contests; whenever he moved to pump past Vukovich, Vukovich would reach out and yank his handlebars, dumping him in a mud puddle.

In the summer of 1956, Parsons turned twelve and got to know race cars for the first time. He learned to drive quarter midgets. The top speed was only 50, but the feel of racing energized Parsons. All the while, inspired by an infatuation with what his father and stepfather did, he had nursed an ambition to drive race cars. "I always wanted to race. I saw what my father did, and I saw what my stepfather did, and I said I want to do that. It fascinated me. Racing seemed heroic." All of his parents frowned on his interest.

In three years of quarter midgets, Parsons chalked up forty-five victories. At sixteen, he went on to Go-Karts, winning in them and developing a brash, aggressive style. In high school, his grades were no great shakes. He would sit in class and dream of cars. He had lots of friends, was an outstanding wrestler, was too small for football. In his senior year of high school, Parsons lost his driver's license after getting socked with three speeding violations during a ten-month period.

Graduating from high school, Parsons moved to California to be with his father, giving himself more opportunity to race. Having quit driving in 1959, his father had taken up promoting races. Parsons plied his skill at three-quarter midget racing, which paid stingily. He also found a job driving a forklift for North American Rockwell, a job he became badly soured on. "It was the pits. I was going nuts. I just didn't care for that job at all. I couldn't believe I was put on earth to lift things." In

1965, Parsons landed his first ride in a full-sized midget, at a track in Santa Maria, California. He set fast time in an ancient car and dusted off many of the local favorites in the actual races. The cars were too valuable, though, and it was another year before someone let him get in one again. His father's win at Indianapolis haunted him. "People expected more of me than I could deliver. My father couldn't hop in the car with me." The years droned on. Three years after he had taken it, Parsons quit his job as a forklifter and applied to both the Los Angeles Police Department and the Fire Department. In school, the few times he had pondered the possibility of not succeeding as a race driver, he had thought he might like to be a cop. The police force accepted him. He had problems with the minimum height requirement. He stood just under five feet eight, the shortest you could be. He did exercises and stretched himself out.

Parsons was a good cop, but he went on whipping cars around ovals on weekends. He climbed into his mid-twenties. Driving sometimes on dilapidated fifth-of-a-mile dirt tracks, like small bullrings. before next to no one and for next to nothing, he worked his way up through the minor leagues, thinking all the while of Indianapolis. "Racing gave me a sense of well-being. It was enormous fun. Driving fast, sliding through turns, smoking off guys. I wanted to win Indianapolis. I never wanted to win it because my father did. I wanted to win it because of what it was." Parsons got a case of itchy feet. Low on experience, high on enthusiasm, he decided after two years on the force to shelve the future, follow his dreams, and become a race driver full-time. What would become of him if he did not make it he had no idea, so he did not think about it.

Summers he lived in Indianapolis and winters he stayed in California, allowing himself a full year of racing. As much as he drove, there wasn't enough money to support himself, and by then he was married and had fathered two children. He was pulling in less than five thousand dollars a year from purses; it didn't pay the bills. He went and worked at any jobs he could find. He worked as a switchman on the Penn Central Railroad in Indianapolis. He pumped gas at a Mobil station. He heaved sick Plymouths off the highway as a tow-truck operator. He shadowed suspects for a private eye. At times, he felt moments of limited destiny. But he kept faith in his skills. He went on traveling, defeating lesser talents. In time, he began to win some midget and sprint car races and to finish high up in Indy car contests at smaller speedways. He stood the odd jobs until 1972, when he coughed and shivered through a frosty winter on the Penn Central, having passed up going to California. He said that was it, and from then on race cars became his sole livelihood.

Parsons makes his home in Speedway, a few miles from the track. The house is a medium-sized brick and wood structure. The driveway is gravel. If Parsons strikes it big at Indianapolis, one thing he plans to do is have the driveway paved. The house has eight rooms, a spacious living room with a console television set (Parsons got it for doing a commercial for a bank) and a stereo shoved against the wall. Hung over the television set is a good-sized painting. The nature of the painting depends on what month you stop by. The Parsons check their artwork out of the library.

Parsons begins slowly, circling the course without going up on the banked curves. After a couple of circuits, he starts moving faster and higher. Bill Finley fishes his stopwatch from the chaos of his pocket. Parsons now seems to be traveling at a fair clip. He is in front of the crew again pretty swiftly, and the second hand on the clock shows the lap took him 52.3 seconds.

"Just over 172," a crewman says.

Parsons makes the next lap at 171—then it can be told from the sound of the engine that he is coming in. Coughing and sputtering, the car blurts into the pits. Parsons brakes down and squeals to a stop, looking not too pleased. He kills the engine and, sitting in the open cockpit, carefully opens his visor as the crew converges from various directions and collects closely around the car. The crewmen apparently understand one another, although their language, to the laity, is unintelligible.

"The car's pushing badly," Parsons says.

"Yeah," Finley says. "I hear you squealing."

"I'm just about getting it through the turn. Man, is it plowing."

"Okay, okay, okay."

There is a lag.

"We gotta do something," Parsons says.

"Let's look at the stagger."

"All right."

"Jack it up."

Much of the practice period is devoted to setting up the car, jimmying the chassis so it handles smoothly through the corners. Handling means more than sheer engine power. A racing car has shock absorbers that can be set loose, so that the car floats and has a more comfortable ride, or tight, to make it steer better. Each driver works out his own compromise between the two aims. Then there are torsion bars, which are the equivalent of steel springs exerting an action on each wheel to distribute the wear on the tires. If the right-front wheel and the left-rear wheel put too much weight on the track, the driver says the car is "pushing" on the turns. It wants to run off of the track and right through the wall. When a car's tires squeal through the turns, you know it's pushing. A badly pushing car is "plowing." If the right-rear wheel and the left-front wheel are putting too much weight on the track, the driver says the car is "loose." It wants to spin out. If you alter the weight of the right front, you automatically alter the weight of the left rear, and vice versa. The same with the right rear and the left front. "It's like a table," John Barnes says. "If you lower one leg, the weight shifts from the other end. Same with race cars."

47

Another way to cure push is "stagger," the difference in circumference between the right-rear and left-rear tire. Fill the right-rear tire with more air and a slight lean to the left comes about, which vastly improves handling. Two-tenths of an inch stagger is normal, imperceptible to the eye but dramatically different to the driver. Besides this, there are three mysterious factors known as "camber," "caster," and "toe-in," having to do with the angles at which the individual wheels are set on the car; the angles are not uniform. These three factors have to be computed to be sure that the wheels stay on the track when the car itself is at an angle and to compensate for the deflection caused by friction. Each presents its own special dilemma. Crews are intensely secretive about their caster and camber angles, guarding them from other teams like treasured family secrets.

The car is jacked up. Finley measures the circumference of the back tires with a steel gauge. He lets air out of the left rear. Barnes asks Parsons about the engine. He seems satisfied with it. "She sounds like she's got some beans to her," Barnes says. The engine is restarted. Its din rocks the air and Parsons goes back on the track.

"Right now, we're worrying about getting up to qualifying speed," Finley says. "You don't want to miss the race. You miss the field, you feel as insignificant as a frog at the bottom of a well."

Tassi Vatis, hands in pockets, stands and waits for the car to go by. While Vatis knows more than most laymen about how race cars work, he does not come close to knowing everything, and when discussions go on about the car, he is not fully in on them. Vatis views himself as cheerleader, arbitrator, banker. Some drivers have written contracts with their owners, binding them to the cars for specified periods. Vatis and Parsons shook hands two years ago and that has been it. All the time, Vatis seals shipping deals worth many thousands of dollars on the telephone, no paper work involved. He doesn't see why it should be different with his race car. One thing he avoids is telling Parsons how to drive the car. "I've never needled a driver. I've never told a driver in twenty-five years as a car owner how to drive. If I did, I would be wearing the helmet myself."

As Parsons makes a slow circuit of the track, Barnes says to Vatis, "This is a 190-mile-an-hour machine."

"We haven't run 177," Vatis says.

A solidly built man, with a full head of tousled gray hair and a cleft chin, Vatis looks like he belongs at the back table of a French restaurant nailing down motion picture contracts. He speaks softly, with a thick Greek accent. Fifty-five years ago, he was born in Greece. He first came to Indianapolis in 1948 as a spectator. He was totally overwhelmed by the place. Up till then, he had never seen anything larger than a quarter-mile track with four or five thousand people looking on. Suddenly, he saw a quarter of a million people in that huge expanse. Vatis knew then that he would return someday with a car of his own and that it would run in the race. Two years later, he bought himself a midget and gave race driving a whirl. For two years, he drove here and there, scaring no one. Married by now, he was being pestered by his wife to cease this foolish pursuit. Realizing his shortcomings ("I don't think I had the proper ingredients to become a top driver"), he quit, hired himself a driver, and started winning races. He won tons of races with other men behind the wheel, and then in 1958, he bought an Indianapolis car. Three years later, he took it to the Speedway. The driver wrecked it. A year later, a different driver put a Vatis car in the starting field for the Indianapolis 500. "I almost fainted." The car broke down in the race, a problem that has dogged Vatis cars. Only two have gone the full distance.

Vatis lives in a plain three-room apartment in a Manhattan high-rise. In his 1974 AMC Hornet (he parks it on the street, a decision that once cost him a windshield wiper during a driving rainstorm), he shoots down to the Wall Street district, where, on the thirtieth floor of a

49

thirty-floor building overlooking the Hudson River docks, are the offices of Trans-Ocean Steamship Agency. The company owns ten ships—freighters and tankers—that float raw materials almost everywhere in the world and bring in revenues of ten million dollars a year. None of this goes into racing cars. Trans-Ocean does no advertising, and being a scrupulous man, Vatis feels it improper to use company money to support his race cars. The money is dug out of his pocket. He is on his third marriage (he has eight children) ; his wife thinks him mad. She detests auto racing and only goes to some of the races because Vatis all but drags her to them. She wonders why he throws away good money on monster cars, to see monster cars go around in circles. Vatis can't really explain. "I have no other hobbies. I really have no other interests besides my business. I have nothing else to relax me. I don't like other sports. I don't care much for music, or theater, or movies. None of that. So instead of playing golf, instead of going out to nightclubs, I spend my money on racing cars."

Every May, Vatis gives himself a month's vacation and takes off for Indianapolis. He stays at the Classic Motor Lodge, a stone's throw from the second turn of the Speedway. He drives over to the track every day, getting there about ten each morning, leaving around six at night. After he leaves, he often settles in the lounge at the motel and puts away some drinks. His companions are usually Bob Bunting, a civil engineer in New York, who exhausts practically all his vacation time working for free on Vatis's car, and Matt Murphy, a tanklike man who drives heavy construction equipment around New York, who does the same thing. As the race draws closer, Vatis worries more and more.

Parsons cuts a lap at 175 and another at 175.4. He comes in. Another conference, and after a short interval, Parsons goes out again. Practice passes like that. Run some laps. Talk. Change this. Change that. Run laps. Talk. Adjust this. Jack it up. Let air out of that tire.

More laps. More talk. More changes. Back to the garage. Work. Roll it out. Run again. Back to the garage. "The work is slow," Finley says. "You run some, shoot the breeze, poke around, and drip by drip, speed comes."

This time, Parsons does only a little better than 174, and when he swerves in, it appears that the changes haven't solved the miseries.

"There's a bad push. I'm fighting the car out there."

Finley nods. "Let's take her back to the barn."

"Good. I'm hungry enough to eat a moose."

"Hello, Tassi," Lee Kunzman says.

"Hello yourself, Lee," Vatis says.

Kunzman squats near the car, watching the work on it progress. He is short, with a quick smile. Several years ago, Kunzman was looked on as a real comer among Indianapolis racers. While testing tires at a track in Ontario, California, he was all but killed in a horrible crash. For some time, his left side was partially paralyzed; he was hobbled by double vision. It was unknown if he would ever drive a race car again. Once he did, some of the promise wore off. A crash like that has to do something to a man. Kunzman's face is raddled with rough, red scars around the eyes from burns he suffered in a different racing accident. He has frankfurtery fingers.

"It really looks good," Kunzman says. "You've got some great ideas there."

"We hope so," Vatis says.

Kunzman is ride shopping. Inevitably, more drivers come to Indianapolis than end up racing cars. Paying their own way, dozens of drivers show up with driving uniforms and helmets and stick close to the teams with unassigned cars. They strike up friendly conversations with the owners and work up a lather of reasons why they should be in the cockpit. Above all else, they remain visible, like bums reaching for a handout. Ralph Liguori, a driver of little distinction, has come to the track with eleven thousand dollars cramping his pocket. He raised the money by running newspaper ads and by throwing parties, begging for capital to sponsor him at Indianapolis. Money came in, mostly in twenty-dollar lumps. He has spread the word that his cash will choke the wallet of any owner who gives him a wheel to turn. Some drivers always find they have to pour personal money into a car if they are to drive it, a practice known as "buying a ride." Liguori not being much of a driver, his eleven thousand dollars doesn't stir any interest outside of Internal Revenue. When a car is available, word spreads rapidly through Gasoline Alley. It is out that Tassi Vatis may stick the backup car of Johnny Parsons on the track once Parsons is qualified.

A fuzzy-haired driver named Rick Muther sidles by as Kunzman is chatting with Vatis. Muther is shopping himself.

"What're you doing?" Muther asks Kunzman.

Kunzman, wearily: "Same thing you're doing."

"Jesus, I feel just like a whore," Muther says.

Vatis looks at him, knits his brows. "What're you guys saying, with all the good cars around."

"But yours is the best, Tassi," Muther says. He grins.

"Very good," Kunzman says. "Very smooth delivery."

They all cackle.

★★★★★★★★★★★★★★★★

The infield.

While the race cars swirl and roar around the rectangle with hypnotic effect, skirting between one another and straining their engines, clumps of people loiter in the infield, a vast area of grass and dust ringed by the track itself. Every day that the big course is open for practice, vehicles trundle into the infield by the hundreds, jamming in there in every possible way to park on the clay and grass. U-haul vans. Family automobiles. Aging muscle cars. Hearses. Converted school buses. Jacked-up hot rods. The sun is rising now, falling through a rip in the clouds over the boiling sea of people. Voices holler from cars as they pass; an immense conversation seems to be going on. Wickedest of all is the grassy stretch that curls around the inside of the first turn, a rolling scrub of land that goes under the name of "Snake Pit."

Even on this, the eleventh day of May, only a practice day, nothing like what it will be race afternoon, the scene is wild. Motorcycle parked alongside motorcycle. Children frolicking. Frisbees. Football games. Rock music. Men lusting after women. Beer. Marijuana. Kissing. Sodden mattresses lashed to the roofs of dented old Chevys. People sprawled in lawn chairs, rasping ice. Couches stripped of legs, foam rubber protruding. Portable barbecue ovens set up, franks and burgers cooking. Girls spread-eagled out on top of their car hoods. Buttons reading: GIRLS WANTED—NO EXPERIENCE NECESSARY; I'M WITH STUPID; LET'S HAVE AN AFFAIR. Young mothers with infants strapped to their backs. Beach towels smoothed out on the grass. A vast sea of blue denim (blue-jean shirts, boot-top Levi's, bib overalls). Bathing suits, halters, tied-up blouses. Glistening stomachs—lean, fat.

Two teen-aged girls flounce by. They are pert, with soap-cleaned good looks. Four men are haunched on their motorcycles. "Whooo-ie!" one of them whistles. "Want a lift?"

"You're missing a few buttons," one of the girls sneers, shifting the spearmint in her mouth. They keep walking. The men prowl elsewhere.

On the roof of a 1958 Plymouth, two stereo speakers nude of cabinets are propped up. Ten teen-agers drive their hips at each other to the seething rhythm of rock music. ("Baby, it's the end now, oh yeah.") The music covers the air, drowns out the blatting of the race cars whirling past. ("It's the end, yeah, it's the end, oh, yeah.") The motion becomes more and more abandoned. Admiring the group is a man with a face that is a playground of unsymmetrical bumps. "Youth," he says, wagging his head from side to side. "Youth."

A saffron-faced man, shirtless, nudges his head out of the back of a rusty van. He smiles; he has crooked teeth. "What's happening?" he says absently.

A man with his hair knotted in a ponytail is hawking oil paintings out of a beige van. Spread out in rows are a dozen or so paintings. They are mostly scenes of action —football and hockey. He paints a new one—two cars sliding through a curve—as five people look on.

Four high school girls, all barefoot and in worn cutoffs. T-shirts. A Thermos jug full of beer. A bucket of Colonel Sanders.

"You know, toenail polish melts in the sun."

"Yeah, I know."

"Look how red Sally's hair is!"

"I want it to get redder."

A tall, sardonic fellow in shirtsleeves, a potato-chip hat angled sidewise on his head, takes a long pull at a pint bottle of whiskey. "Ah'm from Kentucky," he yells. Then he takes another pull.

A curious audience. A mixture of ages and faces. Some of them seem to have a mystic feeling for engines, wheels, drive shafts, pistons, and all the other exotic bits and pieces that go into a powerful race car. Others admit to nothing more than a simple desire to be in on a tremendous party, an annual opportunity like no other, to let everything go and to carry on in a high old way. But what difference? There are hardly any good vantage points for infield ticket holders anyway.

Amid the merrymakers, putting up with it all with stoicism, Margaret ("Mom") Gray sits in an orange and white beach chair, hard by the chain-link fence that keeps the spectators from getting too close to the track proper. How to describe her: she is a short, bosomy woman, her hair the color of sulfur, her eyes sleepy and droopy-lidded. She has on a straw sun hat; a red and white umbrella is clamped to her chair arm, further protection against the hot sun. Resting on her lap are a clipboard, a timing chart, and two stopwatches. Seventy-two years old, a cashier at the Indianapolis zoo, she takes off all of May and shows up at the track. Everyday she settles at the same spot in the first turn. She first came in 1927.

Two men sidle over. "Who's running fast?" one of them asks.

"Johncock," she says, peering at her chart. "I got Johncock at 185."

"Who's in car 65?"

"Dickson."

Later, she explains: "I used to drive the cars fast myself, zip all over the place like a maniac, so you understand why you see me here. I like to sit alone. I feel that as long as the boys are on the track, they're part mine. Once they're off the track, they belong to their wives and all. I want to be alone so when they make mistakes I can fuss at them."

Up until 1964, Mom continues, she didn't show up for the race itself. She felt that with all those people she would have little opportunity to see the drivers very well. In her house, she would twist on a radio to the race broadcast in every room; then she would march from room to room and listen to the race. Friends wheedled her into coming in 1964, and "it would take a casket now to keep me away."

A racer bolts past. "Hey, Olivero, get down. Get on down. You're too high."

She rolls her eyes up into her eyebrows. "I tell you, he knows better than that."

Mom claims no favorites. "They feel more like a family to me than anything else, and you don't separate your children. Maybe the ones who have been here longest you separate a little. Root a little more for them. I always like the rookies, 'cause this sport needs new blood. I like the rookies, but they're all my children. I can't ever expect to give up coming here, you know. No sense at all in that. There's just no better place to die than here."

At a quarter to five in the afternoon, with a mild breeze blowing through the track, Eddie Miller, a rookie, goes into the beginning of a big skid toward the infield. Miller is in the middle of completing his rookie test. His last lap was 167 miles an hour. Bolting through the turn very high, above the packed-down rubber that provides good traction, he veers out toward the cement wall. By now he probably ought to lock it up, flatten the tires, and hopefully drift gently onto the grass. Instead he tries to steer his way out of disaster, tries to fool with the totally unpredictable nature of a racing car out of control. He works the wheel furiously, but the car begins to bounce and plow through the infield grass, like a power lawnmower gone wild. It hits a drainage ditch, catapults high into the air, stands up catlike, rolls end over end, clears an inside retaining wall and then a fence protecting spectators. Wheels, parts fly off. Even in the air, Miller is turning the steering wheel. Drivers can never believe they have no control over their machines. The car narrowly flips past a tree; had he struck it, Miller surely would have been dead. Finally, it comes to rest upsidedown, its back wing crumpled, just in front of a small bleacher half full of spectators. Three wheels have been sheared off; the entire rear end of the car is flattened. The damage is total and irreparable. Emergency crews cut Miller out of the cockpit. Miraculously, he is conscious. Later, it is determined that he fractured two vertebrae in his neck; otherwise, he is all right. He'll probably race again in a couple of weeks.

Thirty-one, Miller is not much experienced in race cars. He has driven mostly low-powered sports cars, nothing remotely approaching the immense power of the Indianapolis racers. It comes out that he bought himself a ride with a sponsor armed with twenty thousand dollars and a thirty-two-thousand-dollar insurance policy on the car (ten-thousand-dollar premium) from Lloyd's of London, probably the only firm foolish enough to insure a race car. Surveying the damage a day later, a Lloyd's of London representative is asked how a company decides on insuring a race car. He says, "It's about like flipping a coin."

The two buildings of Gasoline Alley are long, stark, cinder-block structures. Forming a wire-fence enclave inside the track, the buildings are pale white with gray roofs. In all, there are eighty-eight garages, each a compartment not much bigger than a horse stall. Overalled mechanics are poking away at the metallic bugs, searching for speed. Voices ring out from unseen places. An engine kicks up, whines shrilly, then putters out. Another pierces the air. Some of the doors are closed. A guard at each entrance searches clothing for the identification badge that signifies permission to enter. Number 65 is the garage of Johnny Parsons.

"You know, I built myself a cup of coffee and never took the cup," Bill Finley says, and he shakes his head like a groggy fighter trying to clear his brain.

He limps over to a table, hoists a Styrofoam cup, and drains away the contents in two gulps. He knocks some mud off his shoes. Clearing his throat, he says, "Ah, my mind is finally waking up. I think I know who I am." It's eight in the morning.

The interior of the stall is white and bright, like a hospital operating room, and the light from three fluorescent ceiling fixtures glimmers down on the shovel-nosed race machine. His T-shirt already tattooed with grease,

John Barnes is working languorously over the car's rear end.

"You look tired," Barnes says.

"I am. I am," Finley replies.

He blinks. He takes off his wire-rimmed glasses and polishes them with a handkerchief. "Some people figure getting a car running is just a lot of black magic," Finley says softly. "A bunch of witch doctors get together, one throws in a bat's wing, another heaves in a lizard's toe, and they stir up a brew called victory. That's ridiculous."

Finley is an undistinguished-looking man of medium build and height who does not put much stock in personal grooming. He has a small moustache, and his hair is oily, balding at the crown, uncombed. The middle tooth in his lower set is missing. Clothes seemingly fall on him, remaining however they fall. He is a blunt man whose expletives are often laced with speech. Though not usually talkative, if the subject is race cars, he seems in no hurry to shut up. Finley came out of York, Nebraska. When he was young, the family took off for Lakewood, California, and there he immediately got hooked on auto racing. He built his first race car when he was nineteen. Then he wrecked it. He started driving midgets and sprints, having small success. To feed himself, he was a plastic mold maker and a tool and die maker. On the side, he slapped together race cars. He had no books or teachers. He looked at cars, searched his mind, and whacked away. "I learned the trade by sweat and desire. I learned because I wanted to learn." Finley slowly acquired a great technical knowledge of automobiles and the physics of speed. In 1955, he quit driving. "I wasn't making a living at it. I thought if that was all there was to it, do something you know well. I figured if I couldn't do better, the hell with it. Fuck driving." By 1960, Finley found it possible to make a living strictly by building race cars. Two years later, he came to Indianapolis as a crewman on the car of Tassi Vatis. He had built racers for Vatis. "Damn, if I didn't decide to move right away. I decided this was where it was happening. I was impressed by the people. I wanted to be with a car that would win the race. I still want to."

Finley lives a few miles from the Indianapolis Speedway in a plain, ranch-style home. He works year-round for Vatis. Everything in his work is pointed toward this race. Finley readies cars for all of the other races in which the Indy cars compete, but he sees these as dress rehearsals for Indianapolis. "You do something here, and you go down in history. It doesn't matter as much at the other joints. I kind of live for this place." A few yards behind Finley's house is a low, gray, roughcast garage that Finley threw up himself, and where he spends most of his life except for Mays, when he all but sleeps at the Speedway. He works fourteen hours a day, from six-thirty to eight-thirty, seven days a week. Now and then he steals away for some Sunday-afternoon television. His wife hardly sees him. To the question, "When do you take a vacation?" the answer is, "How do you mean a vacation? I go racing, that's a vacation." Finley's garage brims with cabinets and shelves and tables choked with thousands of parts, drills, saws, wrenches, sanders. A black and white poster hangs crookedly on one wall. It says, "Decisions. Decisions!" and shows a small puppy confronted with two fire hydrants.

"If it weren't for me, this place would be a sewer," Barnes says.

"I like messes. I work well in messes," Finley says.

"This is more than a mess. This is a landfill."

The garage at the Speedway has a wooden workbench along one wall. There are these things on it: a Mr. Coffee machine (ten cups, five minutes), a package of filters, a can of Maxwell House coffee, a container of Valvoline Gear Oil, some pipe, a spray can of Mac's Leather and Plastic Cleaner, a transistor radio, a dolly, a rearview mirror, two cans of Mac's Spray Degreasing Compound, masking tape, a can of Mac's Waterless Hand Cleaner, a box of Ideal Clamps, a red vise, a container of N–S

Safety Lock Wire, a hammer, pliers, a pair of Rayban sunglasses, a stick of Wrigley's spearmint gum. Tacked on the wall above the bench are two large glossies. One shows John Barnes scratching himself. The other shows a woman dressed in a bikini penning a moustache on a Johnny Parsons poster. Someone has put a moustache on the woman. On the rear wall of the garage is an electric clock bearing the inscription, "Ask for Valvoline Oil." A small refrigerator is in the corner, full of sandwich meat and beverages. A Shopper's Fair grocery cart is parked near the back wall, its purpose to lug around parts. Against the wall opposite the workbench is a tall metal closet, in which Johnny Parsons keeps his uniforms and Barnes stores his Kenwood stereo. Barnes can't live without music. He feels there is a relationship between music and the way he works on a race car. He flicks on the stereo and moves the dial. If he can locate some Art Garfunkel, it will improve his day. There he is, crooning of romance. Barnes smiles. If the car doesn't go like mad today, it never will.

A chunky man with forearms as thick as Popeye's, a shock of brown hair, a bristling moustache, and great thoughtful eyes, Barnes was born and raised in Indianapolis. He once hoped to drive race cars. "You have to make a choice what you're going to do with your life. I didn't have the opportunity to drive. So I got into this." Lolling around the Speedway in 1969, he met Finley and before long began to work for him. "I'm not like Bill at all. I have a social life. You become very stale if you do nothing but fidget with cars. Bill uses this a lot as a refuge." His voice trails off. "It's hard sometimes. You work and work, and you don't get credit. The driver is a god, and you're in the background. Let's face it, though, the driver's the one who sticks his neck out. He's the one who gets in there and runs 200 miles an hour. I wouldn't do it. I wouldn't trade jobs with him."

He peers at a spark plug, then screws it into place. "I don't want to work on these things for the rest of my life.

I want to keep at it till the cars win and win; then I think I'd like to get into politics. I want to do something for a lot of people. But I want to win. I want to win Indianapolis. My football team here was a winner. I played defensive end. We were undefeated three straight years. Won fifty-six straight games. My whole background has been winning. I don't want to keep losing here."

Barnes and Finley get to the track every day around seven. They check over the car. "You have to go over the whole car from end to end to make sure nothing's broken," Barnes says. "There is a dark side to this business, and the dark side is men getting killed. So you don't cut corners." They heat up the oil in the car. They check the tires for the right pressure. They change the spark plugs. They warm up the engine. Before they leave every night, they lift off the body cover, so now they place it back on. By this time it is nearing noon, which is when they like to practice.

As much as possible, they try to explain what they do to the car to Parsons, though there are often profound gaps in the knowledge of the workings of the car between drivers and mechanics. Parsons has said, "My job is to turn the wheel. It's not to turn the wrench. You give me a race car, and I'll drive the wheels off it. I don't know how to fix it."

Mournful howls murmur from the stereo. Barnes goes over and switches the channel. Carol King oozes out. "Part of this job is to be a funnel from the driver," he says. "To get the information from him on how the car's running and then to translate it into adjustments on the car. Different drivers have different ways of explaining things, and it takes a minimum of a year working with a driver before you're on the same wavelength. Communication is very important. The driver-mechanic relationship is like a seeing-eye dog leading a blind man along the street; he's got to be a reliable guide."

Barnes spends vast amounts of his time puzzling out suspension adjustments, work that borrows from applications of trigonometry and physics and advanced geometry. Computers have been consulted to help in chassis design. Barnes works in his head and on paper. Ideas will strike him, and he will grab a pencil and paper and sketch out a thought. On paper comes a line drawing that would give Al Capp ulcers but is artwork to Barnes. There is no telling when notions will zoom into his head. He might sit up for hours trying to solve a problem, and nothing. The best ideas sneak up on him. Once he was watching television late at night in his motel room, a few nights before a race in the Poconos. The car was running sour. Suddenly, he was struck by a burst of brilliance, a minute chassis change that could make the car fly. Paper and pencil. Scribbles here and there. Next day, the car flew. "The basic idea is to pretend you're the car. I forget that I'm a human being and begin to think the way a car would think if it had a mind of its own. I'll be saying to myself, 'Now, if I shifted some weight in the back from the left to the right side, how would I feel going around the first turn? How would I feel going down the straights?' Then I might come back and say, 'No good. No good at all. I don't feel right. I feel like I'm going to wallop that first-turn wall, and that's going to hurt. Don't shift that weight on me.' And so I'll figure something else out. It sounds insane, but that's the way I work."

Finley scoops up a turbocharger vent that doesn't fit properly. He snatches hold of a mallet that could level the World Trade Center and pounds the vent. Thump. "Damn if this thing won't fit!" He takes another whack. He pounds hard. Thump. "Getting there. I is getting there." Resting, he mops his brow with a handkerchief and looks out through the garage doors. He takes a puff on a Salem and watches the smoke course out through the doors.

"On the mechanical side the work never ceases," he says. "It goes on all year. I'm hammering away in my garage. The range of work is enormous; the volume of parts to be made is tremendous. A wing's cracked; the brakes need replacing; the fuel cell's no damn good; need another fucking windshield. The cars are so complicated today. It used to be one man could do everything out here. One man and a metal monster. Now we don't make anything but minor adjustments on the engine. We send it over to an engine man in town; all he does is fix race car engines. John does the chassis work mostly. I do fabrication. A lot of race car parts are just like those on a Buick, but they got to be lighter and at the same time they got to be stronger. So they're all custom-made. We don't even paint the son of a bitch. Send it over to Bikini Studio. They clip us for seven hundred and fifty dollars to paint it. Three coats. Got to paint the bastard about twice a year."

Helping work on the car are Mike Herion and Butch Meyer, both in their early twenties. Herion is towheaded, painfully shy, likes working on the car because, "I just like racing." He used to perform odd jobs for the state, then was hired to work during the racing season for Vatis. Butch is chunky, with wavy brown hair. He sort of moves like jello, flowing along. He races jalopies, sliding around dusty ovals, works in the garages for extra cash. He sees himself someday in the cockpit of an Indy racer. He has some heritage to follow. His father, Sonny Meyer, is the engine man for another team, one of the best engine men in racing. His grandfather, Louis Meyer, lives in retirement on a farm. Three times Louis Meyer won the Indianapolis 500.

Finley grabs hold of part of a wing brace and starts toying with it. He puts one in mind of a model builder, surveying the progress on his Robert Fulton steamboat or his Boeing 727.

"You know, the name of the game with a passenger car mechanic is to just get the damned bastard fixed as fast as possible. Time is money. Here the thing is to take your time and get it right. Don't be careless—a guy's sticking his neck out. We would take days to fix something a passenger car mechanic would knock off in hours. The closest thing to what we are is an airplane mechanic. You take a passenger-car man—I don't care who the hell he is—and bring him to the Speedway, and he won't know what in hell to do. Of course, you take me and put me to work at the Mobil station and I'll be walking the streets in no time. I'll be taking a week to replace a muffler."

A crewman from another car struts in, a strong, heavy-thighed man, his broad face wearing a sullen expression.

"How are ya Bill?" he says.

"I don't know," Finley replies. It is his stock response to the question. "What're you doing?" Finley hollers.

"Trying to find some miles an hour."

"They're out there."

"That's what the kid says. He can't find them."

"How fast you going?"

He squints. "173. Stuck at 173."

Finley puzzles a moment, pausing and cocking his head. "Better hire a detective."

To reach this moment in this garage, probably more than three hundred thousand dollars has been spent—money chipped in by Vatis, automotive companies, and sponsors. The chassis costs about forty thousand dollars, bought from All American Racers. Engines, with accessories, go for around thirty-five thousand dollars, from Drake Engineering. A set of brakes fetches two thousand dollars. If you hope to win, Indianapolis demands spares. Tassi Vatis has brought three chassis, three engines, and a mountain of parts that could be whipped into another engine if necessary. You only run an engine seven hundred miles before it is rebuilt at a cost of about fifteen hundred dollars. A badly damaged engine could cost fifty-five hundred dollars to repair. Usually a car is practiced and qualified on one engine, which is then rebuilt for the race. Besides this money, there are salaries for two full-time mechanics (Finley and Barnes) and two helpers (Meyer and Herion), air fares, rental cars, towing expenses, motel bills, meals, a truck to cart the cars to races, insurance, long-distance calls, painting, lettering, entry fees. Everything takes money. The costs of this kind of racing have rapidly escalated recently, such that they are nearing the point where all car owners lose money; 50 percent of the purse is Vatis's (40 percent goes to Parsons, 10 percent to Finley), and it is never enough to offset his expenses. In the early 1960s, good cars were brought to the track, prepared, and run in the race for not much more than twenty-five thousand dollars. A. J. Foyt estimates his effort now consumes a million dollars. "So," Finley says, "you can see where the chances of some Cinderalla winning get less bright every year."

At four o'clock the car is rolled out to the pit area. The air is calm—perfect condition—and the sky cloudless. A lot of cars have been on the asphalt. Johnny Rutherford, Al Unser, and Foyt have all turned laps over 189 miles per hour earlier in the day, several miles an hour quicker than anyone else has managed. The crowd has an electric hum. People are talking. There are crackles of laughter. There is a slight delay in practice as a squirrel is shooed off the track.

Parsons worms out onto the track and quickly builds up to speed. Within two laps, he is running over 178. Then he snarls in. The engine chops and dies.

"So. How was it?"

"Felt better. A lot of the push is gone."

"How was the boost?"

"About seventy. I think we ought to raise the boost and get more power."

"Yeah. Okay."

"Maybe we should reduce the stagger a little, too."

"Okay."

Finley and Barnes crook over and make the adjustments they discussed, and Parsons glides back out. After a warmup lap, he makes a circuit at 180.4, his first in the 180-miles-per-hour bracket.

Barnes swirls around and shouts to Vatis, "Hey boss."

Vatis darts a look at Barnes. Barnes shows him the pit board with 180.4 chalked on it. Vatis lets loose a smile. Before he completes another lap, Parsons comes in. He says he still thinks there's too much stagger and not enough boost. The crew tows the car to the garage to work on it.

Around five-thirty, it is brought back out, fired up, and pushed onto the track. Immediately, Parsons clocks a lap at 184.5, his best lap by 4 miles per hour. Two more laps at 180.7 and 183.3. Then he hurtles in and kills the engine.

Smiles are on the faces of the crew as Parsons wiggles out of the car.

"There's still some push," Parsons says.

"Front wing, do you think that helped it?" Barnes says.

"Nah, mostly the front tire."

"Okay, did you notice if we got our proper boost?"

"Nah, it looked like we didn't even change it."

"Okay, let's go back to the house."

So far, only a dozen drivers have turned laps over 180 miles per hour. Parsons, with his clocking of 184.5, becomes the eighth-fastest driver in practice. Faster, in fact, by .125 miles per hour than defending champion Bobby Unser.

★★★★★★★★★★★★★★★★

On a flawless morning, two days before time trials begin, Jan Opperman finds himself in his garage choosing the design to go on his race car. One design portrays a small fish, the Christian symbol for man, with "Spirit of Truth" written in block letters above it. Inside the fish's belly is a cross. The other one depicts a bigger fish with "Spirit of Truth" lettered neatly inside the stomach. There is no cross.

"I think I like this one," Opperman says, fingering the design with the lettering inside the fish. He has long, thinning hair and beaky features, and is wearing a flowered shirt, Levi's, and moccasins. On his left hand is a diamond ring, which he got for winning the country's richest sprint car race a few weeks ago. It must be rich to hand out diamond rings. Strapped to Opperman's belt is a small leather pouch with a cross on it.

"Okay, Jan," says a large, barrel-chested man who is jacketed and tied. He came up with the designs.

"It's got more grab to it. Doesn't seem like we got to have the cross in the design."

"Okay, Jan. We'll plow ahead then with this one."

"Praise the Lord," Opperman says.

Opperman is an ordained minister—a preacher on wheels—who would like to use auto racing as a way to scatter the word of Jesus. Up till recently, he had a reputation around the tracks as a druggie. He made no bones about using every drug to come into his hands. Grass. Hash. LSD. Uppers. Downers. He did everything but push needles into his arm. Bent out of shape over life, Opperman had the idea that drugs might "lead me to a better truth. Love was what I was after. I never experienced love." Then one day Opperman "bumped into a Christian who had so much love. I felt so good about him that I gave him some hash. He said, 'I've got something better if you just listen.' I did. He had something better. That something was Jesus." Suddenly sold on religion, Opperman began to give up drugs in favor of the church. "It didn't happen all at once. For a while, I used to go to church stoned all the time. Jesus catches His fish before he cleans them."

Thirty-eight, Opperman lives out on a one-hundred-fifty-acre ranch in western Montana, hard by the tiny town of Noxon. On the ranch he has built a log church where he preaches a couple of times a week. His church is called "Us Concerned Racers for Youth on Solid Rock." His congregation numbers around thirty-five. Drug addicts being converted are put up in the church. By rustling together money from "fellow Christians and others who want to get the truth out," Opperman hopes to bankroll a racing team that can tramp the country preaching for Jesus. "I just want people to know I love Jesus Christ, and I'll do anything I can to further His gospel. The race car is like a church. It's something people look to. I want people following the car. I want to have revivals. Have a real major racing ministry. I have some fantastic gospel singers, hard acid rock musicians who are former addicts. I want a truck to go around to the races with them. Have Jesus rock music concerts. Then I'll minister to the people. Racetracks are just a tremendous harvest field. They're all ready and waiting."

Opperman scratches his leg. "I've drawn some ridicule. A lot of people don't see how religion and racing can go

together, and they use this as a way of condemning my
beliefs. All my preaching and practice in Jesus means
love. Love fits anyplace. There's a need for love in racing.
And I feel privileged to bring love here. I'm just doing
a job like anything else. Like digging a ditch. Some of
the guys don't like me. They think this is all a lot of
bull. But God says is you don't get persecution you're not
doing His job."

Standing up, Opperman looks at the untended race
car before him. It's burnt orange, looks like a squashed
tomato. "Gosh, where is my mechanic?" he says. "This
car needs some work done on it." He pauses. "The
mechanic on the car is a bit up in years. Seems to be in
his seventies. He doesn't move too fast. I hope he's been
praying."

Opperman folds his arms across his chest. "You know,
I really respect race drivers. I think the race car driver
and the trapeze artist are the most strained athletes. The
strain is tremendous. And trapeze artists and race car
drivers get killed; the others just get knocked down a
little. It's a tough sport. The others are tough, but this
one takes your life. Every driver is on the edge of death
every moment, from the best man on down. Death is
just a nick away. When a car is running right, it's wonderful. When it's not, it's an animal. It scares you out
of your wits. As you get older, you begin to respect these
things. You begin to respect that they'll take you right
away."

A crewman sitting opposite Opperman says, "But with
the Lord on your side, Jan, how you gonna get hurt?"

Opperman bites his lip and shakes his head. "I'm not
afraid any longer," he says. "The fear of death isn't
there. The fear is of wrecking the race car and not getting the job done. When you get right with the Lord, the
fear trip is all gone. He's not gonna take me."

Reaching behind him, Opperman rubs his back. "I've
got quite a sore back. Most race drivers have hurt backs

and necks from crashing. You pay a price to drive these things."

In high school, Opperman was a quarterback on the football team. One day, he busted a shoulder and couldn't play any more. So he started riding motorcycles. "I've owned a car since I was eleven. I was always totally crazy then. I would drive at insane speeds. I'd spin a doughnut on a narrow road. You could kill yourself doing that. A few of my friends did." After high school, he started racing professionally, working on the side as an iron worker and a pilot instructor. In the summer of 1971, Opperman learned something of the ugly side of auto racing. His younger brother, Jay, was killed in a racing crash in Iowa. "He was passing this car, and it came out on him and flipped him over the fence. He never had a chance. Jay was a better driver than I am. But he hadn't learned much when he was killed. He drove on nerve and guts. The two of us struck a pact. If either of us got killed, we vowed there'd be no tears, no thoughts about hanging it up, no funeral. Just go on." Opperman wears a tattered cowboy hat that had belonged to his brother "to sort of carry the torch." A bear tooth dangles on a chain around his neck. His brother gave it to him and told him to "run like a bear."

Running like that, Opperman has become just about the best sprint-car driver there is. One year he won forty-four features. But the money is poor in sprint cars, and Opperman would like to race only Indy cars. His beliefs have made it difficult. "A lot of owners blackball me," he says. "They don't want me in their cars as long as I preach what I do. They're just narrow-minded people. If I could only win. I would love to win this race, so I could get more money to spread the word of Jesus."

" 'Lo Jan," a mechanic from another car says, poking his head in the door.

"Hey there, brother," Opperman says.

"How she running?"

"I'm afraid it's gonna take the Lord's blessings to make this thing go. It's up to Him. I'm praying. I say, 'Help. Father, why don't you help us out.' "

There is a lot of commotion in the pits. Janet Guthrie, the first woman to try to get into the Indianapolis 500, is heading out for some practice laps. Guthrie is a media happening. Reporters and cameramen follow her like a shadow. Rows of spectators—beefy men, women beside them—jam around her, craning for a look. All the headlines in the local papers go to her, even if she doesn't appear on the track. She takes a lot of needling.

"Janet, hey Janet. My wife would like to try this too. She's had quite a good deal of experience in Volkswagens. What do you recommend?"

She just walks, smiles.

"Janet, are you really going in that car by yourself? All by yourself?"

A New Yorker, Guthrie is thirty-eight, single. Her hair is brown, her face pleasant. She's raced in a lot of sports car events, though never anything this big. The daughter of an airline captain, she holds a degree in physics. Off the track, she works as a consumer-information specialist for Toyota. "Racing killed my career in physics," she has said. "And it's pretty much killed my social life. But I'm just totally committed to racing."

Guthrie got here because Rolla Vollstedt, a Portland, Oregon, lumber executive who has been bringing cars to Indianapolis for fourteen years without winning, wanted a woman in one of his racers. Friends mentioned Janet Guthrie as the best woman driver around. Many of the male drivers think it doubtful that a woman has the strength to run the 500 mile race. Bobby Unser has said he "could take a hitchhiker, give him a Corvette from a showroom, and teach him to drive faster than Janet Guthrie." Guthrie knew she was getting into a male-chauvinist bastion. "I am a racing driver who happens to be a woman," she says.

The big thing is, Guthrie's car is old, neither fast nor durable. It has spent most of the time under repair. She hasn't even been out enough to finish her rookie test. It's a common problem for a rookie. In auto racing, equipment is half the game. Tennis rackets, golf clubs, and baseball bats make up 5 percent, maybe less, of what is decisive in their sports. Hardly anything is more terrible for a driver than to see the death of his car, to sit there and watch all the arrows on the gauges flicker to zero. You have no control over what's happening to those pistons behind you, though one could burn out and knock you out of a race. You have no control over those tires beneath you, though one could explode and stuff you in the wall.

Guthrie sputters out and turns some laps in the low 160s. Nearby, like wound-up toys, a line of cars crawls onto the track. When she comes in, the car making a racket, there is a wild, old-fashioned rebel yell. Then a spectator hollers over from the fence: "Hey Janet, you gonna get in this race or not?"

She looks over briefly. "I'll be in it," she says.

★★★★★★★★★★★★★★★★

A cloudburst. Rain. Buckets of it. It pelts down, thunking on the roofs of the garages, and washes with a deeper tone on the concrete. Dark clouds extend to the horizon. Friday. The final day of practice before time trials start. But no practice seems likely. At nine o'clock in the press headquarters, track superintendent Clarence Cagle, the man in charge of the day-to-day operation of the track, slouches up to a microphone propped on a round table with a backgammon board stenciled on it. Track officials have come to talk to the press about the preparations for the big race. Around fifty reporters and cameramen jam-pack the drably furnished room. Free doughnuts and coffee are being served. In his late fifties, Cagle is a lean, bespectacled man whose head has the proportions of a lemon. He began his working life as a common laborer on a farm owned by Tony Hulman's father and has been at the track since 1945, living in a small clapboard house just outside the second turn and staying so busy that he has yet to see the race.

"I feel like the mayor of a city," Cagle begins. "Everything you have in a city you have here. Babies are born here, probably conceived here. People die here. Weddings are sometimes decided on here. Almost every sort of facility and almost every sort of problem exists at this track."

74

His year-round staff numbers a hundred and five people, mainly construction and maintenance workers. Yet when the Speedway opens its gates for practice, the staff balloons to almost a thousand people, and then on race day it rockets to three thousand six hundred, supplemented by three or four hundred people who agree to pitch in for nothing. The people who work in Cagle's city: they come from almost everywhere, and they are almost everyone. All of them earn the minimum wage, though money is not why they come. "They all want to be close to this race," Cagle says. Presidents and vice-presidents of big corporations come; also lawyers, doctors, college professors, farmers, accountants, a circus juggler, airplane pilots, plumbers. A man used to rumble in from Alaska, Cagle says, until he was voted mayor of a town there and civic duties got in his way. A retired race driver shows up from Hawaii and starts inspecting race cars. For thirty years, a Miami dentist has closed up shop in May, told his patients to go easy on sweets, and come to work at the track. Millionaires appear, whose time is gold. During May, they pocket the minimum wage—$2.10 an hour—just like everyone else. Cagle welcomes a good number of college students to the work rolls, though he warns them stiffly that he will fire them if they cut classes or if their grades suffer. Teachers at schools in the area let Cagle know how the students on his force are making out, and almost without exception, he has found that grades shoot up in May. "I figure they want so much to be a part of the race that they slave extra hours at the books," Cagle says.

Then Cagle plunges into the minutiae of his beloved project. It takes three thousand gallons of paint to paint the plant, he says, and ten years to lay down a single coat. Ten thousand chairs are painted each year, a gallon of paint covering eight chairs. In late March, a hundred tons of fertilizer goes into the ground. To mow the lawn all at once would require five hundred and forty hours of labor. Two thousand two hundred and forty man-hours are needed to sweep the stands and set up the seats. Three gross of brooms are wiped out. Just painting the four-inch white line that runs around the inside of the course consumes seventy-five gallons of paint. Enough toilet tissue is used to run a twelve-foot-wide layer completely around the track. If you took the length of the pits (two thousand feet by fifty feet) and dumped all the Coca-Cola drunk during the month, there would be a river of Coke a quarter inch deep. Enough hot dogs are ingested to compose a hot-dog link that would run nine times around the track: twenty-two and a half miles.

The track's fire chief, Cleon Reynolds, a garrulous man in his fifties, strides up to the podium. He speaks in a hammering voice. Under his control is a staff of two hundred and fifty firemen and twenty pieces of moving equipment, enough to douse fires in a good-sized city. "It takes a hundred and fifteen men just to man the pits on race day," he says. "We have three firemen assigned to each pit and then, every five pits, we have other people who are available to fill in whenever they're needed. . . . Fire here is different from a lot of places. With gasoline, there usually is smoke and flames available. But when you have burning alcohol, you have to know what to look for to even see it. We can't have people working who don't know there's a fire until they feel the heat and it starts burning around them. When there's a major fire on the course, the biggest problem is getting the men out of those sunken cockpits. The Nomex suits will only protect a man for thirty seconds before his skin blisters. If a driver inhales flames, that's it. We've got hydraulic tools to pry the drivers loose."

Then loudly, "I'm just like the rest of my people. After all the years I've been here, I still get nervous and uptight. For the first twenty-five laps of the race, my stomach just churns and churns."

The conference continues. Dr. Thomas Hanna, general practitioner in Indianapolis and the Speedway's medical director, speaks next. A corpulent, soft-spoken man with a big expressive face, he says, "We have to serve a dual function. In other words, we have to protect these men out on the track in the race cars, and at the same time try to protect the three hundred thousand plus people that are in the stands and on the grounds. Anyone who steps inside the gates of the Indianapolis Speedway is our responsibility until he walks back out the gates." Fifteen hundred injuries are suffered during the month, four or five hundred of them coming on race day. To treat them, the track maintains a volunteer staff of two hundred and eighty-five doctors, nurses, and inhalation therapists, working out of a central hospital in the infield and seven first-aid stations spaced around the course. Nineteen ambulances and two helicopters are at the ready; a helicopter can fly someone to a downtown hospital in four minutes, landing on the roof. Hanna details the nature of the problems: nine or ten coronaries are treated at the track; two or three women go into labor; bites occur with regularity—from squirrels, from chipmunks, from dogs, from people. One year, Hanna says, a group of people brought a pig to raffle off. A drunken women sauntered by, examined the pig, and decided she hated it. The feeling apparently was mutual. The woman kicked the pig. The pig all but amputated the big toe of her right foot. Another year, a man stumbled into one of the first-aid stations without his right ear lobe. He had gotten into a fight and a man had bitten it off. The physician wondered why he hadn't brought the ear lobe in to be sewn back on. The other man had swallowed it. Once a spectator flipped a lighted cigarette from high in the grandstand. As it tumbled downward, a man bent over to tie his shoelace. The cigarette fell in his ear and lodged there. His ear canal had to be treated for second-degree burns. Once a security guard drew a long, pleasant draught of smoke from his cigarette. Then he screamed. A bee had settled on the cigarette. The stinger had to be removed from the guard's mouth. Once a man suddenly slumped over in his grandstand seat. Those sitting next to him thought he had been struck by metal flung off a car. It turned out he had been wounded by a bullet. Several youngsters had been target shooting a few blocks from the track. One of them missed. The man was all right.

The worst disaster, Hanna says, struck in 1960, when a man built a makeshift grandstand in the infield out of a thirty-foot aluminum-and-board scaffold. The scaffold was guyed to a two-ton flatbed truck; people were charged five and ten dollars to sit on it. As the parade lap got underway, the hundred or so spectators who had paid craned forward for a closer look. Over went the scaffold like a child's overbalanced plaything. Two men were killed, seventy others injured.

A psychologist is included on Hanna's staff, and he gets calls as well. People drift in depressed because their favorite dropped out early in the going. They are told there will be other races.

"You want to know what the most common problem is?" asks Hanna. "It's cut feet. Fans go all over the place in their bare feet, and before you know it, they step on glass or beer cans. We have a mob of tubs set up in the hospital, where we wash the feet and tape them up. Nobody gets out until he's got shoes on."

Then Hanna says, "You take a town of the same size and every medical problem that would occur there on a given day will happen here, except there will be more, because people are coming in a holiday mood and are thus more accident prone. Many of them are boozed up or high on drugs. Who can tell what they will do? For one day, we become the biggest emergency room in the world."

Three o'clock, rain still blistering down, dumping buckets on the track, and the crew on Johnny Parsons' car is sheltering inside the garage, swapping small talk. Water slaps against the wooden doors. With them is

78

Parsons' father, his hair snow-white, his face copper-colored from the sun, just in from California for the time trials and the race. So far in practice, fifty-eight laps have been put on number 93, twenty-nine at speed. The best lap has been 184.4 miles per hour. Although some cars have turned two or three times as many laps, the crew is confirmed in a good mood.

John Barnes says, "A lot of cars are worse off than us. It's not just laps. It's knowing what you want. A lot of drivers take longer to get to know what they want than Johnny does."

"I figure we'll qualify top ten," Tassi Vatis says. "Maybe seventh or eighth, tops. I think we can run as fast as 186."

"It's amazing what happens out there on qualifying day, no way about it," Barnes says. "You can't believe it. The driver gets his adrenaline going, and he picks up speed he's never found before. We've had a driver find six or seven miles an hour on qualifying day. You ask him where he got it, and he tells you he pulled it out of his pocket."

Johnny Parsons says, "I think it's possible we might even sneak into the second row. It depends on how the car works. It would be nice to sit in the second row."

"Qualifying you're getting the sizzle not the steak," Bill Finley says. "Race day you find out what a driver can really do."

Barnes says, "You never know what will happen out there on qualifying day. You can't figure it. We may not even qualify."

Garage-area consensus has it that the pole sitter, the man on the inside of the first of the triple rows as the cars line up for the start, will be one of three drivers: Johnny Rutherford, Al Unser, or A. J. Foyt. Of the three, Foyt seems to have the most backing. Every day he's been running fast, though a touch slower than Rutherford and Unser. There are suspicions, however, that Foyt is storing away a few miles per hour. Foyt denies it, saying, "I've been running just as wide open as a barn door." But then, psyching out the competition is a big thing at Indianapolis. Run some slow speeds and say, well, that's about all you can do. Turn the fastest lap, then climb out and complain that if the car doesn't get running properly, they might as well load it up. Some teams plant phony tips to confuse the other cars and waste their time. A driver will run a hot lap, then point out that he's got a strip of black tape on the rear wing. Helps the handling. In no time, black tape will show up on wings all over the pits. Of course, it won't do anything.

The rain subsides. Breaks of blue open in the skies. The track is dried, and late in the day, it's open for practice. Many race cars are towed out to the pits to crowd in final practice laps; several machines rumbled in only yesterday and have mustered but a couple of laps. Number 93 is taken out to the packed pit lane, the engine fired to life (exploding into a shaking that causes a chattering series of reports like a machine gun), and the car shoved out onto the track, where it weaves its way into the press of traffic. Parsons does three laps and pulls in.

"It's running hot," he says.

"Let's take a look at the plugs." This from Barnes. He yanks out the spark plugs with a long-handled ratchet wrench, surveying each one closely as it is dislodged. Finley peeks over his shoulder. The engine, a new model developed for this year, is designed to pump out fifty horsepower more than the older model. Around a dozen cars are running the new engines, and most of them have encountered problems. A lot of the engines have blown.

"They look all right."

"Let's try again."

Parsons spurts out and turns three quick laps, including one clocked at 185 miles per hour, his best speed. Over the loudspeakers come even faster laps. Al Unser—187.344. Ton Sneva—186.027. Johnny Rutherford—

188.077. Parsons barrels in, the car is checked over, and he turns five more laps, working up to 185.2. Then on the sixth lap, he kills the engine as he swishes by and glides into the infield in the first corner. His crew scampers down and pulls the car back.

"It was starting to seize. The engine was starting to seize," Parsons says, speaking loudly to be heard over the rumbling of the cars. When an engine begins to seize, it usually means it is about to blow.

"Let's take her back to the barn," Finley says. "We'd better operate on her."

The car is gone over. Nothing is found wrong. Finley looks over at Parsons and says, "The track's still open. Do we dare take it down one more straightaway?"

Parsons: "Let's do it."

Barnes: "Let's do it."

With twenty-five minutes left to practice, number 93 spills onto the track. Twenty-nine cars are lapping the oval, filling its full length as if it were race day. The audience that has braved the weather to watch is roaring with delight. The sun is getting lower, not yet red. There are a few clouds. Barnes and Finley clomp over to the pit wall to watch for Parsons. A car goes by. Another. A minute passes. Two. There is no sign of him. Three minutes. Four. Still no sign. The yellow caution light winks on the traffic signal in the first turn, slowing the pack of cars down. The loudspeakers squawk: "There's a tow-in on car number 93."

The wrecker drops Parsons' car off at the pit entrance. Parsons is still strapped in the cockpit. Finley bustles over.

"There was no oil pressure," Parsons says. "She was going."

Finley turns and hollers over his shoulder to Barnes, "It's the motor, John. John, the motor's shot."

All signs of gaiety vanish. Glumly, the crew straggles back to the garage. Finley picks up the phone and calls the engine man. Though his name is actually Walter

Howell, he goes by the nickname Davey Crockett. "I've got some news you're not gonna want to hear, Davey," Finley says. "We lost a motor." "Work still needs to be done on the spare engine," Crockett says. Maybe he'll have it done tonight. If everything went well, the crew would be able to install it in time for trials. The crew starts to pull the broken engine from its housing.

The draw to decide the order for qualification attempts is being held in front of the control tower, the stark steel-and-glass loft on the infield side of the starting line. Leaden skies. A chilly wind. Numbered pills are being shaken in a small blue pouch, the sort in which miners squirrel gold nuggets. In street clothing, drivers and crew chiefs wait in line. They are milling around nervously amid a murmur of voices and terse clearing of noses. A great deal is at stake. The numbers to get are the lowest and the highest ones. Early in the day and late in the afternoon, the air is cooler. Engines generate a lot more horsepower when the air is cooler; the temperature at the Speedway drops as much as twenty degrees between midday and late afternoon. This can affect lap speeds by as much as three miles an hour, a decisive margin. The blind luck of the draw can have a potentially profound effect on who gets into the race.

As they wait for the draw, the men are joking with each other and swapping banter in the style of race drivers.

"Number one's a waiting in there for you. She's all yours this time."

"I'm gonna draw five hundred. I know I'm gonna draw five hundred."

"There ain't no five hundred in there."

"Don't matter. I'm gonna draw it."

"Hell, I got the smoothest fingers in town. My fingers can smell them numbers. If I don't come up with a good one, ain't nobody who can."

"If every number but one had been drawn and you was up, you still wouldn't draw one."

Forty-two cars—the ones that have cleared inspection, been on the track, and run competitive laps—are eligible to draw. As the drivers reach in and yank out the pills, the track announcer hollers out the numbers for the benefit of the several hundred fans gawking at the proceedings. The numbers are then chalked beside the driver's name on a big chart. The draw takes twenty minutes. Bobby Unser—three. Gordon Johncock—seven. Johnny Rutherford—fifteen. Mario Andretti—eighteen. Al Unser—twenty-nine. A. J. Foyt—twenty. Dick Simon —one. Johnny Parsons—eight.

★★★★★★★★★★★★★★★★

The first day of qualifications is the first day the track has drawn a big crowd. Today's Indianapolis papers are bubbling with speculation about which drivers will get in, which won't. How much speed will it take? Who will snatch the pole? The pole sitter—who is determined on this first day of qualifications—pockets a cash prize of twenty thousand dollars and a bunch of subsidiary prizes; for instance, a thousand-dollar traveler's check from Citicorp and a watch. His chief mechanic is named Mechanic of the Year and is given a breakfast in his honor. The fastest cars on the grounds, therefore, usually try to make the race the first day. This particular day has brought at least a hundred thousand fans out to the course.

At ten in the morning, an hour before attempts are scheduled to begin, rain again slaps down on the track. Dark portentous skies droop overhead. Rain is predicted all day. The Speedway is a flat, drear panorama. Unmindful of the dour weather, mechanics and helpers are scrabbling about, working on the race cars. Interstitched with the pelting of the rain is the whine of engines being tested as crews ready cars in case the skies clear. The garage area is crowded: packs of people shuffle through, peering at the racers, chatting with great animation, asking each other who their choices are.

Texas Garland is a big, shambling man. Middle-aged, with a voice of rooster-crow penetration, he is a heavy-equipment operator in Indianapolis who, in his spare time, works on the crew of Johnny Parsons' car. Texas is hunkered outside the garage on a wooden folding chair, and he leans back so that the front legs come up off the ground. "It's gonna rain till Tuesday," he booms. "It's just gonna rain till Tuesday."

He would like it to. Inside the garage, number 93 roosts on a metal table—no nose, no cowl, and most importantly, no engine. The new engine wasn't finished last night. It has yet to arrive. Bill Finley is at the engine shop working furiously on it with Davey Crockett. As it is, when the engine does get here, it will still be a matter of hours before it can be bolted in. Anyone who has his hopes pinned on number 93 wants rain.

"Ain't nobody gonna trial today," Texas says archly. "Look over at them clouds. No wheels will turn today."

Tassi Vatis smiles thinly. "Let's hope you're right." Vatis is tramping up and down outside the garage, the doors of which are flung open, showing off the disassembled machine inside. In the garage, John Barnes is silently arranging tools on the worktable, so when the engine comes it can be dropped into place as hurriedly as possible. He mops his face. "The pressure here is like a pendulum," he says weakly. "It swings back and forth. One week it hits you; one week it misses you. Today it seems to have hit us."

Now a loop of new weather comes through, and the sky begins to show signs of clearing. The wind has backed. The sun finally breaks through the flat overcast that has been brooding over the big track.

"Hey, Bunting, do your rain dance," Texas says.

Bob Bunting, Vatis's friend from New York, is slouched against one of the garage doors, as though waiting to board a bus. He looks at Texas and then pans his eyes across the sky.

"Come on rain."

"It's gonna rain till Tuesday," Texas says. "I know it is."

"I hope the sky knows it," Shorty says.

The sky begins to darken and some drops fall.

"We're gonna be saved," Texas says. "We're gonna be saved."

It is only a few drops. The sun comes back out, and the sky begins to clear of clouds. Activity intensifies in the garages. Mechanics are as busy as geese. Over the public address system, chief steward Tom Binford announces that the track will open for practice in an hour and forty-five minutes, with qualifying starting a half hour after that.

"Rain," Texas says, looking morosely at the sky. "Why don't you rain?"

Vatis slurps a cup of coffee. He and Texas trade bleak expressions. He continues his nervous pacing.

"Finley, I think you better get here," Texas says.

Johnny Parsons sticks his head outside the garage. The sky roars for a second. A plane, sunlight at its wing-tips, climbing, lost now in the middle of the clear day. "I can't believe it's gonna clear up," Parsons says. "Rain. Rain."

The burr of the phone. Barnes picks it up. "Okay. Okay." He hangs up.

"He's done. He's on his way over."

Bunting says, "Well, we're gonna find out just how fast you can plop an engine in a race car."

Cars are being rolled from their stalls out to the pit apron. Gasoline Alley begins to dissolve of crews and spectators. Cars not in their assigned spots when the trials begin must automatically fall to the rear of the line. By Speedway rules, cars that qualify on the first day start ahead of those qualifying on the second day, who start before cars qualifying on the third day, and so on. Slow cars, no matter when they qualify, are "bumped" from the field, so the thirty-three fastest machines start the race. If Parsons has to qualify tomorrow, he will have to start further back in the pack than if he had qualified today.

Five minutes before the track is open, Finley shrieks into the garage area in a pickup truck, an engine in back. He brakes down and squeals to a halt. The engine is carried into the garage, and the crew scrambles into action. Wrenches begin to fly. Once everyone is inside, Vatis clamps shut the doors and leans back against them. Parsons sits down and folds his arms across his chest. He sits as though waiting for someone in the lobby of a hotel.

A crewman from another car stops by. "How's it look, Tassi?"

"I'm a hoping," Vatis says, waggling his head. "I'm a hoping. Can you help us out with a little rain?"

Practice begins. A mess of cars take to the track, including all the hot dogs. When they are not driving or making adjustments to their cars, the drivers are clocking the competition, trying to figure out what they have to do. The rain has scrubbed away most of the rubber surface, leaving the track slippery and cantankerous and slower than usual. Drivers call the condition a "green track." Spike Gehlhausen, a promising rookie, allows his car to get away from him and clouts the wall coming out of turn one. The right-side wheels are shorn off. Another racer spins wildly to miss Gehlhausen, narrowly escaping contact with the wall. Gehlhausen is all right. There's extensive damage to the right side of the car. Gordon Johncock, who won this race in 1972, just days after declaring personal bankruptcy, cranks his car up to 187 miles per hour. He's a pole threat. Another fast runner, Mario Andretti, the 1969 champion, isn't around. He's racing in Europe and will have to qualify next weekend.

As qualifications get under way, forty gaily colored cars are lined up, leap-frog fashion, down the pit apron.

Number 93 isn't among them. If Parsons hopes to qualify today, he must go to the rear of the line. The stands along the main straightaway are packed. Murmurs and catcalls and other noises shoot out from them. In the qualifying runs, a driver has the track to himself and turns four laps, ten miles, with the average of the four representing his qualifying speed. Drivers have won from as far back as twenty-eighth, but the advantage of starting up front is that you avoid congestion at the start, far and away the most dangerous moment in an auto race because cars are tightly bunched.

When qualifying, a driver turns speeds he could never maintain for five hundred miles. It's a flat-out run against time, a man and a machine against a clock. Each driver can take as many as three practice laps. Each crew is given a yellow and a green flag, and whenever the car is ready, a crewman waves a green flag at the starter. During the run, if the driver and his crew decide he isn't going fast enough, the run can be aborted either by the driver slowing down and pulling to the inside of the track or by the crew displaying the yellow flag. Each car is allowed three attempts. If there's no wave-off and the car completes the four laps, its qualifying speed is established; the car may not make another run. If the speed turns out to be too slow, the car is out of the race. The driver, though, is free to jump into another car. On the final day of trials, there is usually a lot of shuffling of drivers and cars in a desperate hunt for the combination that will make the field.

The shrill roar of the crowd rises as defending champion Bobby Unser slides onto the course. Looking down on Unser from a tall tower perched above the starting line, dead center of the main straightaway, is Pat Vidan, the flagger. Flagging the Indianapolis cars is incredibly difficult, for so much of the safety on the track is assured by the flags. Pat Vidan is one of the more important talents in Indianapolis.

His tools are seven brightly colored pieces of cloth:

green (go), red (stop), yellow (slow down), black (report to the pits), blue and yellow striped (move over to let a faster car pass), white (one lap to go), and black and white checkered (the finish). A block-shaped man with a muscular build and white hair swept back, Vidan has been waving the flags at Indianapolis since 1962. He doesn't flag anywhere else. As with everything, there is a technique to flagging. "With the green flag, you keep it furled up against the shaft and held in place with the trigger finger. When you're ready to give it, you release the finger and it comes out and you start waving. You always try to wave the green flag with a flourish. You attract the driver better that way, and after all, racing is part show business. You want to please the fans. So you zing it around a little. I get so many women who come up to me and say, 'I just love the way you wave the flags.' With the checkered, you hold it spread open, so the driver knows it's coming, and then you wave it around. You've got to put your all into the checkered at the end of the race, because by that time your arm is liable to feel like jello."

Vidan has studied the shape of the flag, studied the shaft that holds it, monkeyed with the aerodynamics of waving a flag, until he has perfected what he feels to be the ultimate set of flags, the perfect set. No companies exist to turn out flags. Not enough demand. Vidan has his custom-made by an Indianapolis seamstress. The dimensions of each flag are twenty-eight inches by twenty-four inches, the optimum size. Any bigger, Vidan has found, and the flag when waved may end up draped all over the flagger's head. Any smaller and the driver might not see it. The flags are made out of heavy broadcloth. Silk is no good. When struck by sunlight, silk sometimes loses its color. Drivers wouldn't be able to tell which flag is being waved. The shaft of each is an aluminum tube with a wooden rod rammed inside for greater stability. Aluminum alone, Vidan has discovered, bends too much. The bottom of the shaft, where Vidan grabs it, is knurled on a lathe. When Vidan was flagging his very first race, back in Portland, Oregon, it was a steamy hot day. No knurls had been cut on Vidan's flags. The cars swept down the long straightaway, their engines whining, ready for the green. The fans were on their feet. The cars looked good. Vidan brought the green flag up and started waving. He watched as the flag shot out over his shoulder and headed toward the grandstand. The cars flashed by, the crowd yelling, and Vidan stood there waving his hand, as if bidding good-bye to a favorite aunt departing on an ocean liner. Ever since, Vidan has knurled his shafts. He has never again lost a flag.

Bobby Unser takes the green and swishes around to complete his first lap. Timing of the cars is accomplished by electronic clocking devices activated by photoelectric cells. The clocks are calibrated annually by the Naval Observatory and vacillate less than a second in thirty days. Unser has been having his problems. In one week, he has lunched two engines. Around seventy thousand dollars up in smoke. But now he is fast—187.032 miles per hour. Then, abruptly, on the second lap he slows and glides around into the pits. He has just lunched his third engine.

At 3:10 while the track is shut down to clean up the oil spilled by Unser's car, the crew rolls number 93 backward down the pit lane and wheels it into line. It is thirty-eighth. Three hours remain. Unless lots of cars pull out of line and give up their attempts, there doesn't seem much chance of Parsons getting out today.

"Where's my sleeping bag?" Finley says.

"I left it with your tent," Shorty says.

Bunting says, "We could buy some of the cars in front of us and pull them out."

Gordon Johncock fires up and moves out. He does four laps at an average speed of 188.531 miles per hour and may have the pole. He guides his car down the pit road to cheering from the big crowd. Out goes Mel Kenyon. Kenyon was badly burned in a crash at Langhorne,

Pennsylvania, a number of years ago. His left hand was left with stubs for fingers. Kenyon drives with a special glove with a ball socket that fits over a peg riveted to the steering wheel. He takes two warmup laps. Then on the third he loses control of the car as he leaves the second turn, slides for three hundred feet, and hits the wall with a clanking plash of metal against concrete. He isn't hurt. The car is badly damaged.

Johnny Rutherford, the first of the three pole favorites, takes to the track. Everyone perks up. Rutherford takes one warmup lap. Two. Coming around for the third, he gets the green. He powers through turn one and slides up near the wall, using every inch of track. His engine screaming, he glides through the second turn, then whips back out near the wall, not an inch of daylight between his right-rear tire and the hard concrete. In three minutes and nearly eleven seconds, he is through. His average —188.947 miles per hour. Rutherford has the pole. The crowd responds with prolonged applause. After he clambers out of the car, Rutherford says, "There are a couple of guys back there named A. J. Foyt and Al Unser, and they're kind of lurking in the weeds. I'll breathe easier when they're done."

But when Foyt goes out, he is a disappointment. He'd made some changes in his car, and they didn't work out. He qualifies at a speed slow for him—185.261. If he had any miles per hour up his sleeve, it appears he should have taken them out and added a couple more.

"Ole A. J. used to eat the bear," a mechanic says. "Today, the bear ate A. J."

"Well, it's not really good," Foyt grumbles when he comes in. "It's a disgrace to me, my car, and my crew."

"I hope it will handle better on race day," an interviewer allows.

"If it don't, I'll park it."

Al Unser doesn't do much better. He orders some last-minute adjustments that also backfire. He qualifies fourth fastest, barely ahead of Foyt. The final minutes go by,

91

and the gun explodes ending the first day of trials. So many crews flagged off cars or watched them break down that only nine cars managed complete attempts. The front row stands at Rutherford, Johncock, and the biggest surprise, Tom Sneva, a young driver who looks like a junior high school principal from Oregon—which is what he was until he got hooked on racing. Al Unser, Foyt, and Pancho Carter fill up the second row. The crews straggle back to the garages. Parsons was ninth in line when the gun sounded.

"We needed another half hour," Finley sighs.

Walking beside the car, Tassi Vatis says, "The speeds were slower than I thought. Much slower than practice. If we could have gotten out, we'd have been well up. Second or third row. I guess that's racing. By this time tomorrow, we should be in this race."

★★★★★★★★★★★★★★★★

Johnny Parsons dreams a lot. This comes up as he is wiping his goggles in the garage. It is the morning of the second day of qualifications. The subject matter of many of these dreams is the Indianapolis 500. The makeup of the dreams varies, though in almost all of them, Johnny Parsons wins the race. In one, he clocks fast time and goes on to lead every lap of the race, breaking track records almost every time around. He wins going away, the most thorough domination of the race ever seen. In another variation, Parsons doesn't lead any of the first hundred and ninety-nine laps, though he lingers in strong contention. Foyt heads the pack as the cars surge into the final lap, Parsons hanging back in second. Through the first two turns and down the backstretch, it's still Foyt, with Parsons a couple of car lengths back. As Foyt pours through the third turn, Parsons closes to within a car length. Down the short chute, the cars sprint tail to nose. Thundering down for the checkered flag, Parsons whirls inside of Foyt, and side by side, the two burst across the finish line in a photo finish. Parsons, of course, has won by a hair. "The dreams have everything in them," Parsons says. "Me drinking champagne in Victory Lane. The wreath around my neck. The beauty queen. The flashbulbs." Now and then, when Parsons is feeling charitable, he allows someone else glory. He finishes second.

There is an hour and a half of practice before the second day of qualifications begin, and number 93 is towed out to the pit apron to do some running. Sunlight glitters on the chrome and bleaches the asphalt. The engine is started, and Parsons billows out of the pits. As he takes a lap, Tassi Vatis says, "If we run as well as we have been, we should be the fastest qualifier today."

Finley paws out his stopwatch and begins to time Parsons' laps. He stands up and shades his eyes to see the track, like the captain of a ship searching for land. Parsons shrieks past on his first lap at speed. Finley gawks at the watch. A lap of 186.2 miles per hour, the best he has run. Then a lap at 186.3. Barnes is all smiles as he beckons Parsons to pull in.

"Let's stick her in line," Finley says. "That's fast enough. We don't want to break the sound barrier."

"She's stitching all right. She's stitching."

Parsons cruises in, brakes to a stop. The car engine mutters and expires.

As he wiggles out of the car, Barnes pumps his hand. "Way to go. Way to go."

Finley gives him a hearty clap on the back.

"She felt like a lady," Parsons says. "I could run her all over." When a car is really working well, drivers say they can run it anywhere, including on the grass. They say they can attach a lawnmower to the car and mow the lawn.

The crew takes the car back to the garage to get fuel. Twenty gallons are pumped in, half the capacity of the tank, the strategy being to run light in trials, to gain more speed, but not too light or else the car will run loose. With qualification time approaching, number 93 is rolled out and parked in line. The pit area is now crowding up with cars and crewmen and fans. In the stands, the turnout is around half of what it was yesterday. By yesterday's order, Parsons would be ninth in line, but already six cars have pulled out, their crews unhappy with the speeds. Parsons is now third.

Barnes peers at his wristwatch. "Two minutes."

"Let's move her up there," someone says.

Bill Vukovich meanders over and plops some "lucky" gum in Parsons' hand. Parsons pops it in his mouth. "A quarter of a second in each corner," he says.

Parsons is in a good mood. The problems that plagued the car earlier in the week seem, for the most part, to have sorted themselves out. The car should be quick. There is almost an apathy to Parsons. Part of his strength on the track is fidelity to mood. If he is a bit of a ham off the course, he is all studiousness on the track. He is never casual there. And while he may be tense and anxious up till the night before qualifications or on the night before a race, he is all calm when the big moment arrives. "It's like when you're cramming for a big test in school. All the while you're studying, you're nervous and tense. You worry constantly. Then the day of the test comes, and all you can do is concentrate on the test. You haven't time to be tense. You're writing answers like mad."

The car is shoved to the front of the line, and Parsons scrambles in and is buckled down. While he slumps in the car, a crewman supports a board over his head to block the hot sun. Chief steward Tom Binford, clutching a walkie-talkie in his hand, walks over to give him the qualifying instructions.

"You know how we count laps. You come around and across that line—one lap. Second time—two laps. When you come around to finish your third lap, the flag must be dropped by your crew chief in order for you to start your attempt. Otherwise, if nothing happens, it's not a run."

Binford glances up at Barnes. "If you want, for any reason, to flag him off, flag him when he comes by you, not when he's anywhere else on the track. Flag him anytime before he completes his fourth lap."

Binford drops his gaze to Parsons. "And be careful when you come in. Have a good run."

Sitting on the pit wall, Parsons' father quietly watches the goings-on, his face starched with concern. Like an applicant waiting to be interviewed for a job, he can't sit still. He wishes he could get in the car and qualify it himself. "I've been around this track more than him," he's telling himself. "I know how difficult it is. Stay loose out there."

"Start her up," Barnes hollers.

Butch Meyer sticks the starter into the rear of the car, hits the switch, and the engine throbs to life. Exhaust fumes rise in fleecy gobs. Parsons removes his glasses, wipes them clean on his uniform, fits them back on. Binford looks over and motions Parsons to move out. The car lurches and careens ahead down the apron.

Parsons rushes by after one warmup lap and takes the green flag.

From the loudspeakers: "And he's on it. Johnny Parsons into the number-one corner, right on the white line as he goes through the turn, moves up near the wall and then sets her down into the number-two corner . . . off the turn now and heads down the back straightaway— Johnny Parsons—he's at the halfway point of the back straight, getting lined up now into the number-three corner . . . rolls through the turn into the short chute, near the wall in the straight and heads down into the number-four corner . . . Johnny Parsons through the number-four turn, drills down the main straightaway . . . green flag continues to fly . . . one lap complete."

"Whoo-oo-oo-s-s-s-sshh-h-h-h!"

"Number 93, right on the line as he goes through the turn . . . up near the wall in the short straightaway . . . Johnny puts her into the number-two corner . . . off the turn and looks for the northeast corner . . . halfway down the back straightaway. . . . Here's the time on that first lap—49.33 seconds. The speed—182.445."

Vatis's face flashes with surprise. He grows fidgety.

What happened to four miles an hour? The engine again?

The speeds stay about the same. The average for the run is 182.843, which will do, though it is much slower than had been hoped for. For the moment, Parsons will start twelfth. No smiles on the crew as Parsons swerves into the pits.

"It was the engine again," Parsons says. "The engine was going away. I didn't think I'd finish that last lap. We lost several hundred rpms. Just ran flat out."

Finley says, "We're gonna have to make her over."

When the car gets to Gasoline Alley, USAC officials impound the tires it qualified on. According to USAC rules, a car has to start the race on the same rubber it qualified on, and so the tires are taken off every car after it completes its run. Between now and the race, Goodyear technicians will pore over them with x-ray machines to see that there aren't any cuts.

In the garage, the crew dallies around, sipping beer and chomping on chicken legs. The mood has shaded off. There is a flood of relief that Parsons is in. The men are chewing over the run, enjoying some laughs. They slap each other's backs and pat each other's butts and pound and whoop. Music romps through the garage. Parsons says, "Boy, coming out of three on the third lap, the engine was pulling so bad I figured, oh, no, this is it. This is the end. I didn't think I was gonna make that last lap. I was talking to it so bad: 'Please, just stay together. Just live.' "

Barnes heaves a sigh. "Well, at least we're in the show."

Vatis says, "You're always happy when you're in. It's the first hurdle."

Out on the track, the race against time continues. Bobby Unser and Roger McCluskey outqualify Parsons, shoving him back to fourteenth starting spot. Gradually, the field swells to twenty-one machines.

Listening to the speeds being announced, Parsons'

97

father says, "Fourteen's all right. He can take it from there."

"Yeah, maybe," Vatis says, picking his right foot up and putting it on a chair seat.

"He likes that traffic. I used to like that traffic. It's fun."

Finley says to Barnes, "We gotta figure out what's wrong with that motor."

In a big tent alongside Gasoline Alley, under the sponsorship of Ayr-Way stores, a celebration barbecue is being held for Ayr-Way and WIRE employees. Before the day is out, two thousand employees will trudge down the feed line, and they will gobble down ten thousand pieces of fried chicken.

Amid the racket of people, Ayr-Way officials are chatting about why they sponsor a race car.

"There are sponsors out there who spend a lot of bucks and who put their name on the car and that's it," says Al Colgrove, Ayr-Way's marketing director. "We never approach sponsorship from that standpoint. It's a pure merchandising effort."

The chain's creative director, a cheerful, dark-haired woman named Fran Connor, says, "There's a good strong feeling inside the company that this is their car. Whether you're a cashier, a manager, a cleaning lady—it's your car."

She opens a beer can. "Johnny's super from an advertising standpoint. Basically, I think he understands what a sponsor wants. You know, we don't get anything out of the purse. And we don't sponsor a car as an ego trip. It has to carry its merchandising weight the same as any other promotion. In interviews, he always manages to work in the sponsor's name. That can be a hard thing for a driver to do in a straight news interview. We don't want him to be crass. He has to use a lot of finesse. You have to slip the name in subtly."

David Kenny, a smiling man with a beetle-browed

angular face who is Ayr-Way's president, says, "I'm a car nut and always have been. I grew up in Colorado Springs and the biggest thing for me was the Pikes Peak Hill Climb. Some friends of mine and me built a car to run in the hill climb in the early 1950s. We tried two years in a row. I drove it. It was a sports car. We didn't qualify it either year. I was in high school then, and I scared the daylights out of myself several times."

Kenny pokes some chicken into his mouth. "When I came into business here, it seemed to me there had to be some way the retail side could take advantage of all that qualifications and race-day crowd. I sat down with the advertising director several years ago and tried to decide what to do with the 500. And we decided the best thing we could do was to sponsor a car."

Fran Connor says, "There are probably five events in the world that are really super. When you have one of them in your own backyard that really captivates the public, we felt it would be a bad bet not to take advantage."

"We feel the money we invest brings a very good return," Kenny says. "Traditionally, May was not a big month for us. Since we've sponsored cars, May has become a much better month. Business has gone up perhaps ten to twenty percent. We couldn't buy the free advertising we get out of sponsoring a car. It's far more than we spend, or we wouldn't spend it. We tried to measure the amount of editorial mention we get in the various media. We found it astronomical. We probably realize a hundred thousand dollars worth of advertising in a four-week period, for an investment of less than a fifth of that."

The store does all it can on its own to make its presence felt at the track. Fifty thousand speed charts with "Ayr-Way WIRE" on the back are passed out during the month. Fifty thousand biographies of Parsons and the rest of the team. Eleven thousand beer coolers. Ten thousand sun visors. Fourteen thousand Johnny Parsons buttons. Four models work at the track thumbing out all this material. Eight billboards are spaced around the city touting the team. Newspaper ads run almost daily, as do radio commercials. All of the Ayr-Way stores are decked out in checkered flags and banners featuring the race car. A photographer works in the garages snapping pictures of the team to supply to the media and for internal use. The manager of the Ayr-Way store who orchestrates the biggest sales increase between May 7 and May 15 wins choice seats for the big race and a night on the town.

Chugging down some beer, Kenny says, "We base who we want to get by the cost and who the people are. We wanted a particular type of personality. We're a young ambitious company, so we didn't want an aging veteran. We wanted someone with charisma. The driver has to be a representative who will do the Ayr-Way stores proud. Some of the guys out there, you ask them their name and they'll be stuck for an answer. We didn't want that. Johnny is great on his feet. He doesn't stick his foot in his mouth every time he opens it."

Tassi Vatis has never had it easy lining up sponsorship money. Several years ago, he stuffed four hundred letters in the mailbox, addressed to a good chunk of the corporate world, asking for sponsorship money. He stressed that racing is viewed by millions of people. That the car is on the highway traveling between races about thirty thousand miles a year. A race car on a trailer does attract attention. One reply came in. It was from Valvoline. Valvoline sponsored Vatis's car for three years.

One Saturday night, David Kenny and his wife were at a local motel for dinner. This was in midwinter, two years ago. Kenny's wife had gone to high school with Johnny Parsons. The Kennys bumped into Parsons, and she introduced him to her husband. When the Kennys sat down, they got to talking and his wife said, "Hey, why don't you sponsor Johnny Parsons." A short time later, Kenny approached Parsons, and thirty thousand dollars went from Ayr-Way to Tassi Vatis. Ayr-Way got half the money back in the form of free advertising on WNAP, a local rock radio station. This year, Ayr-Way upped the sponsorship to thirty-five thousand dollars and took on WIRE, switching from rock to country.

★★★★★★★★★★★★★★★★

Monday afternoon at the track is dreary. A day for clouds. Layers of thin, gray clouds lie over the track, over the garages, over the grandstands, over the infield. Scarcely any spectators show up at the grounds, missing out on the making of Speedway history. Janet Guthrie wraps up her rookie test, and thus becomes the first woman eligible to qualify for the race. The quartet of drivers serving on her jury agree that her test was one of the better ones they have sat in on. Questioned in the press room afterward, Guthrie says that she is looking forward to building up some speed and getting the car in the race. "I think we're gonna put this one in the field," she says. So far, Guthrie's fastest speed is a shade over 171 miles per hour. That, obviously enough, will never make the race.

There is not much other action at the track, just garage work on the big cars. Fiddling with engines and chassis. Sitting on a beach chair outside one of the stalls, unnoticed, is a wizened man in his seventies with gaps between his teeth. He looks sour. He is George Souders, 1927 winner of the Indianapolis 500. He has been considering, with only minor signs of emotion, the fact that he is perhaps the least-remembered winner of the race still alive. He accepts this as inevitable if not pleasant. Time has not been kind to him. A year after he took the race, he was involved in a serious wreck in Detroit which "damn near bought me the farm." He lay unconscious for nearly six months after the crash. His left arm was never properly set. Nowadays "it fills a coat sleeve, that's about all." He gave up racing, did some traveling, ate through the forty-seven thousand dollars he collected at Indianapolis. He ran a gasoline station in Lafayette, Indiana. He made propellers at Curtiss-Wright. He worked at the Purdue University Airport. He tended the Purdue golf course. A few years ago, a fire blazed through his house trailer in Lafayette, reducing almost everything he had to cinders, his racing trophies included. "Fire don't have no respect for history." He resumed his life in a small apartment.

Souders remembers his big victory as if it were yesterday, even if no one remembers him. "I started in the twenty-second position, a long ways back. Hard to see back there. Was gonna be tough. But I was tough. I was ninth after ninety miles, plowing through that traffic, running like a honey. Made my first gas stop after two hundred miles. Whistled in and whistled out. Before I had to take a second stop at four hundred miles, I was in the lead. I was so far out front that I was able to come in and get filled up and have three tires changed. I could have caught a film and still won her. I finished nearly twenty miles to the good. Was somethin'. Was really somethin'."

But the glory has been fleeting. "I never paid a heck of a lot to that end of it. Glory and all that rubbish. Don't really care much about that. The real sporting fans I care about. They don't forget a man like me overnight. No sir. You ask them about George Souders, they'll remember his big win. Course they'll remember it. Was somethin'."

Near by, Dick Simon is cheerfully working on his race car. He is flanked by two blondish, grinning men in black boots. The special buzz of racing talk creates a pocket around them. A stocky, bald-headed man in his early forties, Simon is possibly the only driver at the track who openly confesses he doesn't expect to win. He is an oddity.

103

"For me, it's a wonderful treat just to be in this event," he says. "It's an honor, really. It doesn't matter if I don't win. It's an honor to finish last." Simon has given up a lot not to win. A few years ago, he up and left a job as the chairman of the board of a seventy-million-dollar holding company. At the same time, he quit the presidency of one insurance company and the vice-presidency of another. Still not finished, he also walked out on his wife. She gave him the choice of a race car or her. He didn't think it was a hard decision.

Simon arrived at Indianapolis to race for the first time in 1970. He mortgaged his home to buy a car and then bought a used engine from another car owner. He had no spare parts. He was broke. He had never raced at the Brickyard before. He figured his odds were kind of slim. His used engine proved to be more like a used used engine, and Simon found out he needed a less-used model if he were ever going to get into the race. He trotted back to the same owner, kicked the gravel, hemmed and hawed, offered to give a check dated the day after the race in exchange for another engine. A shaky check for eighteen thousand dollars was traded for an engine. Simon promptly qualified thirty-first and finished fourteenth. He won eighteen thousand dollars.

What Simon felt he learned that first year was that the critical thing for a man of his limited skill and limited car was to be on the track when the race ended. A lot of cars fall by the wayside, so Simon adopted a "back-of-the-pack" attitude, trying to just keep the car together, not straining it, and maybe he could hit the top ten, even the top five. So far, it hasn't worked. In six races now, Simon has come in fourteenth, fourteenth, thirteenth, fourteenth, thirty-third, and twenty-first. Yesterday, he qualified seventeenth for this year's race.

Knowing he's not going to make it to Victory Lane, how does Simon feel out there on race day? "My hands perspire like a running faucet. My whole body drips water. My stomach churns. My knees won't stop knocking.

A lot of drivers' knees knock, but you don't notice them so much. They're closet knee knockers. I let my knees knock right out in the open. You can hear them all over the track."

Simon is nothing if not determined. In a race at Phoenix once, he was ordered to consult a psychiatrist after he ran the last half of the race with all the insulation ripped away from the water lines that run through the cockpit. His legs were jammed hard against the red-hot pipes, and they were burned down to the bone. But he finished sixth. The psychiatrist told him he had more than the normal amount of willpower. Before falling into racing, Simon was a parachuting and ski-jumping champion. He likes risky sports. "I'm not interested in getting hurt. I like my bones unbroken. I just get a kick out of competitive activities. They're fun."

He looks philosophical for a moment. "I've thrown the whole kit and caboodle into racing. A business career. A marriage. The works. There is just something about the sensation you feel in a racing car at speed that is unlike anything else. It brings out all the good feelings in you. And you can never tell in this sport. Maybe someday I'll finish second or something."

The track by now begins to bring on a feeling of encapsulation; the preparations, so compelling at first, begin to contract the mind. Practice days at the track can seem interminable. The sameness of the laps, the work. During race month, the track dissociates itself from the overlap of events and opinion outside. Gossip in the pits concerns itself with time, who is going fast and who is not, what it will take to make the field. One crewman is saying to another: "I really think that most people here are like me; they are cut off and quite happy to be isolated, if you come down to it." Being at the track suspends time; the heat and noise slow the memory. What day is it anyway? Who is going fast?

Tonight the Monroe Shock Absorber Company is throwing its annual Rookie Appreciation bash at the

Columbia Club, a posh dinner club located in downtown Indianapolis. Drivers, crews, sponsors, press—everyone is invited to applaud the drivers who, a year ago, cracked the starting field for the first time. More than five hundred people turn out. There is always plenty of off-the-track action. During race month, the Speedway crowd meets and communes almost entirely at parties—at parties before parties, at parties after parties, at elaborate affairs held by one of the sponsors, at small dinners given by private enthusiasts in the town's swank hotels. Out at the track, men are trying desperately to qualify their machines. A lot of heartbreak and hairbreadth defeats are involved, forking up an inexhaustible source of conversation at the parties.

The reception room, the focus of which is a large square bar, is a murmuring cave of speculation and rumor. A former winner, so one hears, is on the point of switching rides. Or it is known that a new sponsor is going to plow some big money into a team. The ice clinks and glasses perspire icily in hands.

"What's it gonna take?" a haggard-looking crewman asks a mechanic on another car.

"It's really weird this year. I mean weird. Could be 178 miles per hour. Could be 176. Could be less. I'd be sitting pretty with 180, tell you that much."

Two women, softened by curiosity, lean forward to listen.

"We've yet to see 180."

The mechanic raises a drink. "Here's to your seeing it."

"Foyt might be hot stuff to some people, but he's just another coconut to me," says a freckle-faced, mascaraed woman to a big, strapping man.

The man eats some peanuts. The woman does without. "Sometimes," he says, "you act like you invented auto racing."

The woman affects a sigh. "Why don't you have another beer."

Speeches. Bill Puterbaugh trots up and is handed one

106

of the traditional Monroe jackets that every rookie in the race receives. Fingering it tenderly, he says, "I can't tell you how long I've waited on one of these jackets. God, it's been a long time. I've seen the other drivers walk around and walk around with them on till they fell off their backs. It's just tough as hell getting into this race, and it's all the tougher for a rookie. It's a rough, rough sport."

Another jacket is presented to Larry McCoy. He says, "I wanted one of the jackets bad, too. Meant the world to me. I can't tell you the difficulty of making this race. A good driver has to have a little bulldog in him, and that's especially true out at this place. I'm proud to have done it. I've cried when I haven't made this race. There's a lot of crying the month of May in Indianapolis. I thank all of you, and I thank God, too, because you need Him on your side to get into this race."

The speeches go on. A comedian rattles off a bunch of jokes—some good, some not so good—and the evening drifts away. The dinner disperses. The audience pushes back out the doors and into the dark.

★★★★★★★★★★★★★★★★

"Hey, Johnny, do your name here."
"Sign me, Johnny. C'mon, sign me."
Outside the gate leading to Gasoline Alley, about a dozen people knot and mill around Johnny Parsons, stabbing pencils and papers in his face. Parsons obliges with autographs in a big, flowing script.

A girl presses her arm up to Parsons. "Put it right there," she says. Parsons cradles her arm and signs his name with a ball-point.

Parsons has signed hands, arms, legs, thighs, foreheads, pictures, dollar bills, two-dollar bills, jackets, hats, shirts. Once he autographed the side of a Plymouth.

"Johnny we wish you the best in the race. We really do hope you take it."

And then: "We think we got the winner here. What do you think? I'd say we got the winner. We got a sure winner."

"If he don't lose, we do."

Some older people also crowd in, and they too ask for autographs.

"Boy, he looks good for being a race driver. Not a scratch on him."

"He hasn't raced long enough."

"Boy, you'd never get me to drive one of those things. You'd have to tie me in."

And then: "Johnny, tell me this, you ever take a nip before you go out?"

"What do you think, we go out there sober?"

"Sign me, Johnny. You didn't sign me."

"Put it here. Put it here or I'll scream."

The engine on number 93 wasn't breaking during the qualification run, Barnes and Finley have determined. As it happened, the turbocharger was cranked up too high, causing it to activate a popoff valve which, working like the thing that whistles atop a pressure cooker, regulates the turbocharger boost. When the popoff valve goes off, the car's power is cut down.

"As far as we know, we're going to run this motor," Barnes says. "It's giving fifty more horsepower, so there's no way we don't run it. We ain't here to run dead last."

Finley rubs his cigarette in an ashtray that is overflowing with ashes and butts. "We got the motor out to be rebuilt. End of the week, we'll plop her back in and run a couple of hundred miles on the thing to see if she'll live. Call this a reliability check. If the engine's okay, we're gonna take off like a scalded dog."

Meanwhile, Steve Krisiloff is given Parsons' backup car, number 92. This raises some eyebrows, because for several days now Lee Kunzman has been telling everyone that he has been hired to drive the car. He was doing this merely to scare off drivers who might have come around. From Parsippany, New Jersey, Krisiloff is twenty-nine, a wiry, sandy-haired driver with narrowly set, quizzical eyes and protruding teeth. He quit an earlier car, unhappy with the speeds he was clocking. He has made the race five times, his best finish being sixth. While a reasonably dependable driver, he developed a bit of a reputation early on for bending cars, which troubles Vatis a

109

little. Krisiloff's approach to the race is kind of nonchalant. "It's just another race," he says. "They pay more money here, that's about it."

Number 92 will compete under the sponsorship of Citicorp Traveler's checks, which, to boot, is paying Vatis a "bundle of money" to sponsor Parsons' car during the balance of the racing season. Parsons is a bit nervous because the decals for Citicorp have green in them, a color that he and a lot of drivers consider bad luck. Superstition used to hang over the Parsons household like a cloud. Never get into a green car. No peanuts in the pits. A train passing over an overhead bridge will bring good luck if one crosses one's fingers going underneath. It doesn't count if the fingers aren't crossed. Never leave your shoes on the bed. Never leave your hat on the bed. Parsons doesn't know where the superstitions come from, but he would get it if he didn't abide by them.

Krisiloff heaves himself into number 92 to take some laps in the car. He turns laps for around a half hour. Other than some minor chassis changes, Krisiloff says he's happy with the car. It has an old-style engine in it, but the feeling of the crew is that the car can run over 180 miles per hour.

"You check to see if we can get some new tires?" Barnes says.

"Yeah, Goodyear's supposed to roll some over," Finley says.

"New rubber ought to add some miles."

So much can be gained or lost on account of the tires, and there is always a lot of tire talk in May. Tires come— in unlimited amounts—directly from Goodyear, the sole supplier of Indianapolis rubber. Goodyear keeps a plant just down the road. Goodyear engineers are up and down the pits, temperature and pressure gauges in their hands, checking how hot the tires are when the cars roll off the track, measuring air pressure. The tires are free. The company is glad to have race drivers use them, giving it publicity galore. It even pays the leading teams retainers approaching a hundred thousand dollars to run the rubber, sing its praises. Racing tires used to be a way to test the progenitors of passenger tires. No more. Racing tires, in effect, have gotten too good. Since they cannot run in wet weather, they would make no sense on a passenger car. Goodyear learns from working with racing tires only how to produce a better racing tire.

The genesis of any one year's Indianapolis tire goes back a full year. A new tire is created for each race. It runs only at Indianapolis. The tires are extraordinarily thin, the better to dissipate heat. Teams of engineers run through as many as a hundred sets of tires during the year, sifting to find the perfect set, looking for the best compromise between what produces the fastest speed and what produces the greatest durability. Before a compound is actually tried on the track, as many as thirty-five lab tests and more than two hundred quality-control inspections are done—abrasion, heat resistance, twist, scuff. So exacting are these tests that almost 80 percent of the compounds tried are scrapped before they are ever mounted on a race car. It is unusual for anyone to remain in race-tire development for very long because the strenuous nature of the work takes its toll on a man's family life and on his mind. Goodyear spends upward of a million dollars to develop the Indianapolis tire. Up till last year, Firestone invested as much, competing face-to-face with Goodyear for car wheels. But it decided it could no longer justify the exorbitance to shareholders and pulled out of race-tire building. After the big race is over, leftovers are sold to other forms of racing and to farmers who slap them on tractors. Impossible as it might seem, somewhere in South Dakota a farmer may be tooling along on A. J. Foyt's tires.

A cool now sits over the crew's assembly, an easiness, a sense of superiority.

Bob Bunting says, "Well, it's looking pretty bright now. The new engine looks all right. The backup car is running."

"Let's hope so," Vatis says. He slaps his stomach.

"We're due for a little luck from upstairs."

"That's what it's all about," Vatis says. "You could try for a hundred years, and you could never bring a car here and win this race. Or you could come here once with one race car and take it. We've been here awhile. We're not being hoggish. We'd just like our due."

★★★★★★★★★★★★★★★★

Some have had it worse. In a golf cart outside one garage sits a big, beefy man. He has a square face and heavy jowls, a bulbous nose, discolored teeth, and short, thinning white hair. He is dressed in a blue and white striped shirt, black trousers, and a blue racing cap, and he is wearing glasses with heavy black frames. He is Lindsey Hopkins. No one has pursued the Indianapolis dream as long and hard as Lindsey Hopkins. He is rich, and he has sunk hundreds of thousands of dollars into bringing race cars to Indianapolis. Over the years—since 1951—he has put thirty-six cars in the race; he has not yet had a winner. In 1973, he arrived in town with four cars and put all four into the lineup. ("Tell me, Lindsey," an acquaintance asked. "When you gonna bring thirty-three cars here?") Three of the cars went the distance; they finished third, fourth, and seventh.

Hopkins comes from Atlanta, Georgia, and his money comes from his being chairman of the board of Securities Trust Company and a director of Coca-Cola. His interest in Indianapolis is traceable to 1935, when he saw the race for the first time. The race galvanized him. He decided it "would be a lot of fun to enter a car in the race." In the brokerage business at the time and distracted by other matters, he didn't get around to actually fulfilling his ambition until sixteen years later. "I just got tired of seeing Henry Banks, a real fine chauffeur, driving bad race cars. So I bought him a good car. I haven't been able to stay away from this place since."

Hopkins is a sociable, irrepressible man who is always eager to engage in some "garage racing," rerunning the years of races that have eluded him. "I could have written a lot of history at this place," he is saying. "I had all the makings. All the ingredients. But it wasn't in them cards. No matter what hands I drew, somebody else always drew a better one. I figure four or five times we should have won the race but lost it for one impediment or another." Bill Vukovich (whose son is racing at Indianapolis now) had come to master the Brickyard, winning the race in 1953 and 1954. In 1955, Hopkins signed him to drive his car. Leading the race by such a margin that "he could have made a pit stop for a beer and still won her," he was involved in a wicked crash on the hundred and thirty-eighth lap that took his life. In 1957 and 1959, Jim Rathmann ran second in Hopkins' cars. In 1960, some people from Texas lured Rathmann away with promises of a lot of money and backing in an automobile dealership. He won the race in their car, and "he could have just as easy won her with me." In 1961, everyone believed Hopkins had brought the best car and driver combination to the Speedway. All through practice, his car ran several miles an hour faster than any other. On the day before qualifications were to begin, his driver, Tony Bettenhausen, agreed to test a car of a friend. A five-cent cotter pin on the steering broke, and Bettenhausen was killed. Another year a newspaper blew over the radiator of the Hopkins entry while it was running among the leaders, causing the engine to blow. Bobby Marshman seemed to have the race well in hand in 1966, when he was forced to run off the track to dodge a spinning car; he knocked the plug out of the crankcase, losing all the oil and the race. Not long after, Marshman was killed while tire-testing in a Hopkins car.

114

"This race means more to me than any two races, any three races," Hopkins says. "What a great feeling it would be to win the 500. The crowds, the color, the music. It's like Christmas here. It only comes once a year."

Hopkins lifts himself out of the cart and lumbers into the garage. Raising his head, he nods at a double row of framed photographs on the side wall. "There's my rogues' gallery," he says softly. Seventeen Hopkins drivers peer down from the wall, three of them Indianapolis winners. "Yup, three of them won the big one, but never for me. I put two people into racing as owners. They didn't have any interest until I got talking to them. Both of them have won the race, and I haven't won her yet." Alongside the photographs is a sketch of a magician's hat with a rabbit crouching before it. The sketch appears on all of Hopkins' cars, a tribute to his days as a semiprofessional magician.

Hopkins rubs his jaw, which bristles with rust-brown stubble. He is plagued by skin cancer and avoids shaving whenever he can get away with it. "You have to have a lot of luck to win this thing," he goes on. "Without it, you're dead. I just haven't had it yet." He has brought three cars this year, the one being driven by Roger McCluskey having clocked the fifth-fastest time during the opening weekend of qualifications. The other two have yet to make their attempts. Hopkins always brings more than one car. "You got to work on those odds. This race is like a big craps game. We're all working on those dice. The more numbers you got, the better off you are."

He breaks off, is silent for a time, then settles himself on a stool in the far corner of the garage. He pats his brow with a handkerchief. Will he win this year? "Don't see no reason to come unless you expect to win. It's a long way to come just to run with the pack. We all think we'll win. It's like a two-year-old race horse. We all think we'll win."

No work at all goes on in garage number 1. On the doors, a rusty padlock serves warning to intruders. It is the only garage that is carpeted. Car number 67, white with bright red trim, rests in the middle, sunk into the red patterned rug. It is strikingly different from the race cars lapping the track. Much narrower, with no aerodynamic wing at the back, it squats higher off the ground. On one side, the lettering reads, "The Jim Robbins Company Special." No driver is assigned, which is understandable. The car will turn no laps.

Jim Robbins headed up an automotive-parts supplier based in Troy, Michigan. Back in the 1950s, he started to enter race cars at Indianapolis. They were good cars; he got good drivers. One of the machines sat on the pole in 1955. Several of them led the race, threatened to win it, though the best finish of a Robbins entry was second in 1951. Robbins died in 1966. His son, Marshall Robbins, now chairman of the board of the Jim Robbins Company, kept entering cars at Indianapolis. Racing energized him as much as it did his father. In 1970, with Sam Sessions behind the wheel, the Robbins entry came home twelfth. The car would never again turn a competitive lap. Spending into six figures to put a car in the Indianapolis race, looking down the road and seeing a need for an even bigger bankroll, the company decided it just couldn't afford to race any longer. Racing used to be cheap. Now, as Marshall Robbins would put it, "it takes a wallet a mile thick." To pay tribute to his father and to file his own silent protest against what he felt to be unnecessarily escalating costs of racing, Marshall Robbins continues to enter the car in the race. Every year, a thousand-dollar check arrives at the Speedway office from Troy, Michigan. "Basically, we're saying that we can afford to enter the car," Robbins will say. "We can't afford to qualify it."

Although Bill Spangler, a local mechanic, is assigned as the crew chief on the car, he finds himself with monumental time on his hands during May. "I would expect we do a little less preparation than the other boys," he says. As the race rolls near, he and Marshall Robbins can be found slouched in the tubular beach chairs inside the

116

garage, sipping Gatorade and swapping small talk about how it used to be. Racing fans wander by and wonder how in hell such an old beast like that is ever going to make the race. Now and again, a driver will request a chance to take the car out; Robbins will politely beg off. "I guess there's also the thought stuck in the back of our heads," Robbins says, "that maybe, just maybe, someday the costs will come down, we'll go and do some tinkering around, and sure enough, old 67 will roll onto the track." He hesitates a moment, pensive. "Well, it's just a thought."

★★★★★★★★★★★★★★★★

Weekday dinner at the Sherwood. The Real Estate Brokers Association. A capacious, wood-paneled room, tables for four, cushioned chairs. Forty people, mainly middle-aged, have turned out for the affair. Men are jacketed and tied. There are wives and a couple of children—some of the wives in long dresses, the children looking freshly scrubbed. Guest speaker is Johnny Parsons.

Parsons, his father, and their wives are met at the door by the host for the evening, wearing a suit and tie. Evening, folks, glad you could come. There are nods and hellos. Parsons detests speeches and is inclined to regard them with a big yawn. But there are bills to pay. In May, there are mobs of speaking opportunities if you have something to do with the Indianapolis race. Clad in a blue sport shirt, brown pants, and a black suede jacket, Parsons asks about the possibility of their getting a drink. "Sure. Sure. Sure," the host says. They grope their way to a plastic table and sit facing the swaying shadows at the bar. The other patrons are youthful in manner and imaginatively dressed. Parsons orders a beer; the others go for hard liquor. Hunched over the drinks, they talk about races gone by, about hometowns, and about who used to be a hot-dog driver when they were young and who is running fast out at the Brickyard. The host says they ought to go in, orders another round though only he has polished off the first one, and then springs for the check. Parsons gathers in both beers, and his wife, embarrassed to be spotted cradling two drinks, shoves one of them into his hand.

"This is always the way it is," he says. "The driver carrying all the drinks."

The room is hot and airless. Dinner is roast beef, lots of gravy, mashed potatoes, salad, coffee, no dessert. At the podium, the emcee begins by asking everyone to rise and recite the Pledge of Allegiance. A prayer follows. Then the emcee tells a couple of jokes that are not very good and have no particular point. The public address system breaks down, and a man in coveralls scampers in and repairs it. The emcee is chunky and square-headed, with pouched cheeks and pursed lips. He speaks in a toneless, high-pitched Midwest voice. He lights a cigar, and the flare of the match is reflected back in his eyes. Blowing the smoke from his nose, he tells a vaguely risqué story, which evokes a few scattered titters. He presents Parsons with a rabbit's foot for good luck. Then he hands over a weather detector, so Parsons will know when rain is in the air. He gives him another detector for the president of the Indianapolis Speedway. Then he says to the audience, "We have a real treat for you tonight. Racing, you know, used to be thought of as a place where you'd go out and see a bunch of bums drive some cars." A sprinkle of laughter. "But I'm being entirely serious tonight in telling you that we have a lot of good people in racing. They are educated. They have to be to drive the cars like they do today. They work hard at it. Really and truly, the people at the races are truly great people. Now, I'd like to have you hear one of the fine young drivers today, Johnny Parsons."

A rattle of applause. Parsons strides up to the microphone. He wipes the sweat from his face and neck with a handkerchief. "Thank you," Parsons says. "Thank you for having us over. It's a real pleasure. This year, we're starting one row further back than we did last year. But we have a good car this year. We have real good mechanics. We expect big things. Last year we were running fifth, and we were looking pretty good when we lost the transmission. But my crew really has it together this year, and we expect to be more competitive. I've got great confidence in myself, in my car, and in my team. . . .

"Two years ago, when I made my first Indianapolis race, it was part of a dream come true. I've always wanted to race here, since my dad raced, and I guess that had a great influence. I'm real proud to be in the Indianapolis 500. It's always a thrill to be in the greatest race in the world. . . .

"It didn't happen overnight. I'm thirty-one now. I've seriously wanted to race at Indianapolis since I was twenty-one. It's not a sport where you can go out and practice every day. . . .

"My wife Pam and I have two young boys—Johnny is ten and Jimmy is seven—and they're presently racing quarter midgets, and they just took home some trophies two weeks ago. I sincerely hope they get tired of it when it comes time for them to do it as a profession. I didn't push them into it. But when kids grow up, they're gonna do what they want to do anyway. They want to do this, and I don't think I should stop them."

Parsons motions for his father to come up to the podium and turns the microphone over to him. His father says, "First of all, I'd like to make this statement right here. I'm the proudest man in the state of Indiana right now. My boy, my one and only boy, is in the five-hundred-mile race." The audience applauds.

"I have a little mixed emotions about this. They're going a good deal faster than I ever did. Going into those turns at 200 miles an hour isn't home in bed, you know. You've got to have your brain turned on. It's a lot of strain out there, and I just don't want him to stub his toe out there. . . .

"When I was a boy, I made up my mind to drive a race car when I was eight or nine years old, and my family was all against it. You know, you would go to these family dinners like New Year's and Thanksgiving and the such, and they would always ask the little boy, fourteen or whatever the hell he was, what he wanted to do when he grew up. I got so tired of it. And I said I wanted to drive a race car. 'Oh my God,' they would say. 'That's awful. We'll have to feed you and all.' That made me more determined. What happened is they talked against this for so many years that this made me so determined that I would think about this going down the straightaway. Going down the backstretch there would be nobody near my car, and I would think, 'Remember my aunt told me something when I was sixteen,' and oh I would stand on the gas. I wasn't a damn bit tired then."

Young Parsons invites questions from the audience. A man with a thin moustache and fierce eyes asks if there are any drivers who are "squirrelly," dangerous on the track.

"There are some," Parsons says. "It's really minimized. What with the cost of a machine, it's so expensive that in the process of getting there, the hayseeds are weeded out."

A large-chested man asks if Parsons feels Janet Guthrie can be competitive.

Parsons says, "She can't physically do it. She'll get tired in twenty laps. We don't have power steering in those cars. How many women can outwrestle a man?"

Someone asks where Parsons will finish this year.

"Where will I finish this year? Well, we have a good chance to win it. And I seriously mean that." Much applause.

Topics go by. Parsons always has answers to questions, or if he does not, he improvises. He comes off as a regular guy.

Someone asks if there are more drivers qualified to race than there are race cars.

Parsons says, "Oh yeah. There always have been. It's tough to get a ride. I stood in line a long time, walking around the garage area, twiddling my thumbs. It's hell out there."

The questions run out. Applause. It is late. The emcee takes the microphone. Parsons and his father slip back to their chairs. Some of the audience pushes up to the head table and pokes napkins in front of the Parsons to sign. The emcee says how pleased everyone is that the Parsons could come. He says he once had a dream that he was on the front row at Indianapolis. "The dream scared the wits out of me," he says. A ripple of laughter. He says he can't remember the speaker's name for the next meeting, but "I'm sure he'll be interesting." He raffles off a bouquet of flowers. He raffles off a five-dollar bill. He raffles off his gavel. He wins it.

★★★★★★★★★★★★★★★★

One woman looks to be in her twenties, dressed in cream-colored shorts, her shirttails knotted around in front leaving her waist bare. She slouches against the chain-link fence that slants between the garage area and the infield. The rising sun beats down on her. The deep channel of her spine glistens. She has been glued to the same spot for well over an hour, her gaze concentrated on the drivers. Only a few feet away leans another woman, perhaps in her thirties, with cornflower eyes and long dark hair. Next to her is a woman, slightly older, got up in tight, faded Levi's and a halter with anchors on it. In all there are ten of them. Some of them have been hunkering against the fence since dawn. "Pit lizards," "camp followers," "fence hangers" are the tag names they go under.

"Pretty good," squawks a pit man to one of the women as he putters by on a Wheel Horse. "I like what I see."

Her pale, foxy face displays a shadow of weary amusement. She lowers her eyes. He isn't a driver. She isn't interested.

"Ah, you're a wet blanket!" the pit man sneers. He makes a sharp left down the far row of garages.

One of the women is fair-haired and freckled with a hardening baby face, dry, dusted cheeks, brilliant tiger-bronze eyes. She is wearing bib overalls. She has hugged the fence all week, like a teen-ager window-shopping. She looks to be no more than twenty-one. She has had some luck, got to chatting with a few of the drivers, wheedled a drink out of one of them. That is all she will tell. She whispers that she is a secretary from Columbus, Ohio, drove down here alone, will stay through the race. Her sixth year at the track. She makes several of the other Indianapolis car races, occasionally catches a big stock car race. "It depends on how my luck is. It depends on how much of my expenses I cover. May can be the cheapest month of the year or the most expensive. No, I don't like the race. I like the drivers."

Slumped on battery carts a hundred feet or so from the back fence, two crewmen goggle at the women. One of the men is popping bubble gum. His long hair hangs like string in the heat. "Yeah, the women don't make the work here any easier. Makes it difficult sometimes to keep your mind and your eyes on your business. Better off shutting up in the garages. Got to be a driver, though, to really score. Nearer to race day, if the girls haven't been having much luck, then they do get a bit more friendly."

Several of the women begin to drift off and swing toward the bleachers behind the pit apron. They can watch the drivers there as they head out for practice. A fetching redhead, her breath spiced with mint, starts to move away. She clomps unsteadily in a pair of high-soled wooden clogs. She is twenty-five, a librarian from Cleveland.

"Race drivers excite me. I must travel four thousand miles a year following the cars. Guys risking their necks, going so fast—it's really something. I groove on it. Know what I mean? These men are heroes. And I'll tell you, they're nice people, too. Very nice. I enjoy talking to race drivers very much."

She nods hello to another woman down the fence a ways. "I used to go pretty regular with one of the drivers here. Back in 1968, I think it was, he ran a real nice race.

Think he got eleventh out of the deal. Something like that. I never told him this, but the races themselves bore me to death. It's the idea of them that I like. I mean there are just too many laps. How can anyone stand all those laps? And the noise. I wear earplugs. I always have a few beers."

"Yum, babe, you look so good. So good."

Three pit men, one chomping on a plum, sidle past a woman. She wears clothes much washed and faded, has ample breasts, and blonde hair three feet beneath her shoulders. She is barefoot. She rattles ice in a glass she is holding.

"Hey girl!"

"Come on with us!"

"Come on!"

She glances at them, looks from one to the other, stares them straight in the eye.

"What for?" she says. She trundles on down the fence.

Tooling down the alley now comes Donald Davidson. People pound up and fire questions at him about the race. Davidson is the official statistician and historian for USAC, such a famous and infallible fountain of fact that reporters are always approaching him to get the dope. He is both priestly and boyish. When he walks, he moves subtly, like water. If one weren't absolutely sure that Davidson is a human being, one might suspect that he was an IBM System/360 computer in disguise. He has committed almost every fact about the Indianapolis 500 to memory. The complete finish of every race. The highlights of the races. The careers of all the drivers. The mechanics.

Conversation with Davidson is likely to be single-minded. His reading tastes run to almanacs. While the news media and the spectators gravitate to the exceptional—the winners, the fast qualifiers—Davidson is curious mainly about those who never break into the starting lineup and about the comic characters who come to the track. Davidson loves drivers who on the last day of trials are sitting in the last car there is time to clock, who then get the signal to go and the engine won't fire up. This has happened several times. Hapless Bruce Jacobi was entered almost every year from 1960 to 1974. In that time, he made only one fling at qualifying, and it was too slow to get into the show. He is the most unqualified man in Speedway history. Davidson adores him. "George Snider has been the first man to qualify on the first day and the last man to qualify on the last day, yet he still has always qualified on his first attempt," Davidson says. "That interests me." There was Floyd Roberts, a fragment of history who in 1938 wheeled car number 23 from first starting position to first place in the race. The next year, he returned with car number 1, started twenty-third and finished twenty-third. "Just a delightful fact," Davidson says.

Davidson's talent showed up early. As a boy in Salisbury, England, where his father was a film projectionist with a memory no better than a sieve, Davidson started to fool around with toy race cars. His interest went beyond the norm. It became an obsession. Davidson was rotten in school. Classmates would laugh at his report cards. He liked history and did all right in it. He didn't like math and failed it. His mother had gotten outstanding grades, herself having a fabled memory that she used mainly to remember approximately every ballet dancer to ever stand on toes. Davidson, though, would whip through his homework or scrap it altogether to pore over his racing books. In the mid-1950s, Davidson narrowed his preoccupation. He became totally immersed in the Indianapolis 500. Nobody else in Europe at that time much cared about Indianapolis. Many people had never heard of it. "I have no idea why I got interested in Indianapolis. I have never figured that out. I just did." Davidson would save his shillings and send to the United States for Floyd Clymer's *Yearbook*, a magpie trove of facts on the race. He started memorizing the race winners since World

War II. His mind skittered and swooped. He would alight on a fact and gobble it up. He went on to the top three finishers. Then all the winners. Then he decided to drop all restrictions. He remembered everything. Finally, when he started to work as a film projectionist, he managed to store away enough money to make a trip to Indianapolis, where people were amazed by his memory. Soon after, he quit work and moved to Indianapolis. Imagining colossal savings on metal filing cabinets, USAC hired him as its statistician.

Davidson has no idea how his memory works. "I do know I only remember what interests me. I know that I have to see something before I remember it. I can't just hear it. I've also been told that certain types of print are more easily remembered than others. I don't have any technique. I don't read fast. As a matter of fact, I read dreadfully slow." Davidson hasn't limited his sphere of operation to the Indianapolis 500. For instance, he has taken the time to store away all the heavyweight champions and their respective challengers, including the rounds boxed, the site, and the date. He knows all the male Academy Award winners (but is somewhat less reliable on the women). He can, if pressed, recite the winning Wimbledon champions since 1900, along with their losing opponents, and he knows with similar precision the champs at Forest Hills.

Davidson may know a lot about Indianapolis, but he is terribly forgetful about directions. He is lousy with phone numbers. He is horrendous with names that don't belong to race drivers and mechanics. Davidson has always lived in close proximity to the Indianapolis Speedway, near enough that he can walk to it, which he usually does on qualification days and race days, when there are huge knots of traffic. In 1972, he had been walking to the track as usual. It was the last day of qualifications and the crowd was on the thin side, most of the big names already being securely in the field. It was the final hour. The field was full. Davidson had a whole array of new categories

127

of people who had missed the race and drivers who had failed to complete their attempts. He headed home. As he walked, he ran over in his mind the data gleaned that day. It was nice out. He got home. It was a quarter to seven. His wife was outdoors, playing with the children in the garden. She looked up, a frown forming on her face: "Well, where's the car?" The car? Davidson thought. Oh, my god, I drove the car today, didn't I?

★★★★★★★★★★★★★★★★

On the greasy concrete beside the pit wall, the car sits after having turned seven laps at speed. There is the howl of engines from cars ripping around the big oval under the pale, lemon-colored sun. The crew spills out its thoughts.

"The oil temperature went to the sky," Johnny Parsons says.

Bill Finley nods blankly. "She must be going," he says. "Mmmn."

"Maybe we'll have to run another side scoop for the race to get more air to the engine." John Barnes says.

"I don't know," Parsons says. "It ought to be getting enough air." He bats his eyes.

"Let's go back to the barn."

At the garage, the car is hoisted onto a wheeled table, like a hospital operating table, cranked onto it by a winch bolted into the ceiling. The crew has been unable to shake the engine problems that have dogged number 93.

Jim McGee sidles in. He is the chief mechanic on the cars of Mario Andretti and Tom Sneva, both of which are powered by the new-style engines, neither of which has had a drip of trouble. McGee may know something the other mechanics don't, though if so he's not telling. It could lose him the race.

"What're you doing, McGee?" Finley booms.

"Just walking around with my legs crossed."

"Come over here and touch this engine," Barnes says. "We want to give you a disease."

"More trouble, huh?" McGee says.

Barnes nods.

McGee glimpses up at the stereo speakers.

"Nice stereo, huh?" Barnes says.

"Yeah."

"We'll trade you the stereo for one of your engines."

McGee just grins.

"It sure would be great to run this engine," Parsons says to Vatis. "But we don't want to run ten laps." He gnaws at his bottom lip.

"What can we do?" Vatis says. "We run four or five laps, and the engine's ready to blow."

Vatis hasn't yet made up his mind. By this time, possibilities are beginning to pop up in his mind like mushrooms. Run the new engine? Put in an old one? Test the new one some more? He stares out of the garage blankly.

Pam Parsons strolls into the garage, says hello to the crewmen, gapes at the car. "How's it going, guys?"

"Well, if Parsons here can push this thing around at 185, we're in terrific shape," Finley says.

It is all she needs to know. Her knowledge of the workings of race cars is limited. "I can tell you the color of the car, that's about it," she has said.

Pam is perky and pretty. Little scoop nose, bouncy dark hair, a Kewpie-doll smile. Her suit is blue. She is at the track every day that Parsons practices. She settles in the uncovered bleachers behind the pits, following his car whenever it goes out. Indianapolis is the most trying track she goes to. There are the endless weeks of practice to worry through, the qualification days, and then the long race itself. Most of the wives regularly collect at the track, watching their husbands' daily attempts to coax more speed out of their cars. The eyes of each wife are fastened only on her husband's machine. "I always feel

130

that if I watch him," Pam says, "he senses that I'm look-ing at him, even though I know he couldn't possibly see me."

She has grown accustomed to such stuff, living around a racetrack like that. After she finished high school, Pam found a job delivering mail at North American Rockwell, where Johnny Parsons was puttering about in a forklift. A mutual friend introduced them one day, they hit it off, they started dating, and three months later they got mar-ried. They got married twice. A July wedding had been planned, the invitations addressed, when Parsons received notification from his draft board that he was being called the first of June. They trundled over to a judge in New-hall, got married, and Parsons escaped the draft. Six weeks later, they went ahead and had their church wed-ding. "If we had waited to get married in the church, Johnny probably would have ended up in Vietnam."

At the time they were married, Pam had never seen Parsons in a race car. The sport was foreign to her. Par-sons was not driving much then, and she didn't realize how committed he was to the track. "I don't think I really thought he was going to be a race driver. I just didn't think so. He said he was going to, but I didn't believe it. Thought it was just talk, a pipe dream. Then after we got married, he started bringing up the subject more and more often—race cars, race cars—and I realized that was what he wanted to do. I wasn't exactly wild about the idea. It worried me. I liked being more stable. The danger bothered me a lot."

"Johnny, you going to be done early or what?" Pam asks.

"Uh, not sure. Not sure. We got to see what the story is with this engine."

"Well, we can either have dinner at home or go out."

"Let's wait and see."

"We were going to see some friends."

"Yeah, we'll see."

A friend comes over. "How's it going, Pam?"

131

"Oh, could be worse."

"You worrying?"

"You can't worry too much or you'll be a basket case."

"Racing's tough on a wife."

"Yeah, our whole lives are more or less run by racing. When you marry a driver, you marry a race car. It's hard to do anything as simple as take a vacation. You go where the races are."

Pam is eating some potato chips when the wife of another driver, Wally Dallenbach, comes in. "Well, hello there," Pam says.

"Hi, how are you?"

"Not bad. I'm always a little jumpy in May. How's Wally doing?"

"Oh, the car just won't handle. He's fretting a little."

"Yeah, Johnny's got some engine problems."

"Who doesn't?"

"Yeah, what are you going to do."

"I know enough that in May I steer clear of Wally a bit. He gets that look in his eyes."

They stand idly by the car, their faces blank of emotion, as they wait for their husbands.

The drivers' wives tend to stick together. They all want the same thing. They all want their husband to finish up front, and they don't want him hurt. When they sit together, many of them chain-smoke, twist jewelry in their hands, grab arms. Looking at a row of them, it is easy to tell whose husband is out on the track. Here, there, Pam has seen a lot of crashes. "I don't like Indianapolis because it's so hard to see much of what is going on. Whenever there's a yellow light, I immediately think it could be Johnny, and I start looking as the cars come by, trying to find him. I try to keep it in my mind that nothing could happen to him. I know it could. I'm not stupid. When I see Johnny off to a race, there's a big difference from other professions. You think that, oh, he'll be back at five-thirty. But when Johnny goes off, you think something may happen. I go to church every Sunday, and I say a prayer for Johnny's safety every time he races. Lots and lots of prayers are said the month of May."

"Well, I'm going to cheer up Wally," Dallenbach's wife says.

"Okay, good luck."

"I tell you, I think I'm going to be a couple of inches shorter when this is over."

★★★★★★★★★★★★★★

S alt Walther qualifies on the third day of trials. His time is good enough for the twenty-second spot. Walther, at twenty-eight, is the playboy of the track. His personal car is a Rolls-Royce, he wears a diamond ring and a three-thousand-dollar wristwatch, and he lives in a six-figure house with his name painted on the bottom of the swimming pool. His father and car owner heads a large truck-hardware business in Ohio. Walther feels too many drivers lack flamboyance and charisma. He is beautiful in his navy blue tailored driving uniform, trimmed with braid and white stars. His head is encased in a rug of hair. Walther is not very popular in the pits, because he is so unlike the other drivers. Three years ago at Indianapolis, his car brushed the wall and flipped wildly at the start of the race. Landing upside down, it began twirling like a top, engulfing Walther in flames. For more than a month, he lay semiconscious in a hospital bed. One day, the hospital phoned his father and said Walther had just hours to live. Now, on his left hand, he wears a black glove with the fingers shortened to fit his partially amputated fingers. Walther spent endless hours squeezing a rubber ball to recover his strength. He now has more strength in his left hand than in his right.

"Okay, Salt. Okay. Way to go."

"How 'bout that?"

"Show 'em the way around, Salt."

"I'll be grooving."

In answer to calls from his fans, Walther walks to the fence and begins signing autographs. Three teen-aged girls ask if he will have his picture taken with them. They have on short skirts, are a little chunky in the thighs. Beaming, he drapes his arms around two of them while the third one snaps a picture.

"Take some more," he says, flashing a big grin. "No rush. Take some more."

Several more cars join the field. The speeds are quick. Today is being talked of as a "two mile an hour day," meaning that the track is running two miles an hour quicker than normal. The weather is cool, and there's an abundance of rubber on the surface. The first two days of trials were slow.

Mario Andretti, the 1969 champion, churns onto the course with bursts of thunder, and interest perks up along the pit wall and in the grandstands. The feeling is that Andretti will be the race's fastest qualifier, only the ninth time that the fastest man won't be on the pole. In morning practice, Andretti streaked around the asphalt at a speed over 189 miles per hour. It's figured that he's got even more speed hidden away. Sure enough, after an opening lap of over 190, Andretti qualifies at 189.404, the fastest yet. But since he's qualifying on the third day, that puts him nineteenth for race day. As he growls into the pits, drivers and crewmen along the way applaud and lift raised thumbs.

Billy Scott walks into the pits and sits down on the concrete wall. He's just qualified as the fastest rookie in the race. He wiggles free of one of his shoes and tells a race official, "I couldn't believe it. We were real lucky. We went and bought a new engine just the other day, and it made all the difference. That shows you what good equipment does for you. Here I was beating my brains out, and I couldn't run fast. Just couldn't run fast. With the new engine, it was so easy. I couldn't believe it. That's why the sport comes down to who's got the money, who's got the sponsors. It's really not fair."

"You're learning, Billy."

Steve Krisiloff, the driver of the other Vatis car, goes out and qualifies smoothly at 182.131, good for twenty-third position.

After the run, Vatis says, "It's great to have just one car in the race. It's fantastic having two. I'm a happy man today. I'm a happy man. It's a hell of a feeling."

"Should we go ahead and plan on a one-two finish, boss?" Bill Finley says.

"Maybe we should get another car and go for a real sweep."

Back at the garage, Krisiloff comes over to Vatis. "Hey, how much am I getting paid, I ought to ask?"

Vatis reaches into his pocket and snakes out a quarter and hands it over.

"No, come on. Forty percent?"

"Forty," Vatis says.

"Motel bill?"

"What you mean?" Vatis says, acting affronted.

"Ah, I'll do a good job for you. I promise."

"Okay, motel bill," Vatis says. He claps Krisiloff on the back.

Cars continue to race the clock, and soon the entire field is filled. The driver of the slowest car, regardless of what day he qualified on, will now be bumped from the race if his time is beat. In the vernacular of the business, he is the "man on the bubble." Probably several men will sit on the bubble before time trials come to an end tomorrow. Those in the last row are in fear that they will soon find themselves out. They are hoping and sweating.

No more qualifiers show themselves, and so the track is opened for practice. The cars pour out onto the asphalt. One of them booms right back in. The driver gets out and starts stuffing foam rubber behind the upholstery in the cockpit. Apparently the contour is not as he wants it.

Another crew has their entire car up on jacks, putting in a new gear. "The only way to make this thing go is to shove a bomb in it," a crewman says.

Johnny Parsons spills out for more testing of the engine. The crew has made more adjustments and is still determined to run the new-style engine in the race. After a few laps, Parsons comes in. He nearly lost control, the car getting sideways in the third turn, up out of the groove into the part of the track the drivers call the "marbles," from which a driver stands an excellent chance of hitting the wall or spinning into the infield. He cuts the engine and clambers out looking a bit shaken.

"Whew, I couldn't go one lap with the car like that," he says. "As soon as I got into traffic, the car was dancing all over the place."

Barnes says, "Maybe we've got to run more wing."

Parsons says, "We gotta do something. Boy, if we started the race with the car like this, I'd be in a lotta trouble. Good-bye."

"Andretti's running a lotta wing," Finley says.

Barnes says, "Then let's do it."

"We gotta be sure we want to do it. We could try something else. I say we take the car back to the garage and leave it till the morning. I say we don't change anything till the morning."

"Okay, back to the barn."

On the way back, Parsons says, "Boy, I never been sideways in this car. I raised my eyebrows out there. It could have been the wall."

Once I asked Parsons what he thought of the hazards of his profession. We were driving to my motel in Indianapolis in Parsons' van. The radio was playing softly, the Moody Blues spilling out. Parsons said, "You can't be any good in this business if you worry about getting hurt. I'm as aware as the next guy what a race car can do to a person. But I don't give it any thought. Sure, when I see somebody else hurt or killed, I think about it. We all think about it. But when I get in that race car, danger is the furthest thing from my mind. There'd be no point in driving if I worried about getting hurt. You could walk across the street and get hit by an Allied Van Lines. You could get killed in the bathtub. I've flipped race cars thirteen times. I've broken a shoulder blade after flipping a midget at Terre Haute. I hit a rut and rode over the wheel of another car. Flipped about eight times. I was kind of dazed. I was hanging on to the wheel to avoid breaking any bones. I was in the hospital just as an outpatient. I broke a big toe once, when I flipped a sprint car in Cincinnati. On dirt, you get bruised all the time by rocks that hit your shoulders and arms. I used to get my lips bruised. Once I flipped a midget and got a gash in my forehead. Had to have eight stitches. I was dragged out of the car soaked in methanol. Just after I was pulled out, the car went up in flames. That could have been me on fire. One time I was in an Indianapolis car at Ontario, wind came up unexpectedly and it had just started to rain. The car was getting loose. I lost it coming off the fourth turn and was running down the straightaway backward. The car was locked up. It couldn't be steered. I'm backing up at around 110 miles per hour, and then I remembered the pit wall and I'm looking over my shoulder to see if I'm going to hit it T-square. If I did, I'd probably be dead, because the engine would go right through me. I missed it by inches and knocked the nose off the car. I was very concerned. I felt there was nothing I could do about it. If this was the end, well, I was kind of pissed off that we had to run in these conditions. One of the good things about racing and one of the reasons you don't worry much is that when an accident occurs, it's over and done with in a second or so. There's no time to really think what's happening. You're smoking along, and then suddenly, you hit an oil spill and you're in the wall. Before you even realize you're going to hit the wall, you've hit it. Really, I've been lucky. I've never done any sheet time. The other drivers are always kidding me. 'Look at how much I've been laid up and you, you've never put in any sheet time.' Well, I just smile. I figure to race another ten years, and I'm sure I'll put in my sheet time before I quit."

He looked pensive for a while and found an afterthought. "The main thing drivers worry about is mechanical breakdown, something going wrong with the car which throws it out of control. Then there's nothing for the driver to do but pray. Cocktail talk is that drivers must have a death wish to do what they do. That's bull. Every driver probably has a place deep inside him where he is afraid. But it rarely gets to the surface."

Parsons had gotten so caught up in what he was saying that we approached an intersection just before my motel and went right through it. Though he was staring straight ahead, Parsons didn't seem to see the red light.

★★★★★★★★★★★★★★★★

The morning haze begins to lift, and already a restless mood combs through the garages; the crews of cars that haven't qualified have begun to flutter around like chickens tricked by a false dawn. There's no lolling around; everyone's at some appointed place. Hope runs out at exactly six P.M. As an old race hand is wont to say, "It's today or forever dead."

Car 44. Billy Engelhart. Garage 33. A religious program (" . . . and what will we tell Jesus?") spills out of the radio as the car's owner, a husky man with a weary, fretful face, is down on his knees, fiddling with the rear end. The car is sponsored by Lan Hairpieces. The owner, with a pate as smooth as an egg, could use one of Lan's products. Two crewmen concern themselves with the front suspension. Another is digesting the inside page of the morning paper. He is sucking on a banana.

"Boy, they flew yesterday."

"Gonna take some running to crack this field."

"Yeah, gonna need to crank her. He's got to hold his breath and really get his hoof into it."

"Change the plugs, huh kid?"

"Yeah."

"Let's see if we can fire her up."

"Yeah."

140

"Need a bit more room here."
"Give me the speed wrench."
"Got enough air in those tires?"
"Yeah."
"Boy, there is a nice valve."
"Give me the wrench."
"Wrench, doctor."

Car 65. Lee Kunzman. Garage 73. Three men in coveralls are circling the car constantly, like gulls over fish, and then darting in and making their adjustments. In street clothes and sunglasses, Kunzman slouches against the wall of the garage, mutely watching the work.
"You check the stagger?"
"Yeah, I checked her."
"So how is it?"
"Good. Same as we run yesterday."
"Pass me a screwdriver."
"Here you go."
"We need a lot of speed. Lot of speed. A good day to run, though."
"The last day's never a good day to run."
"Got a point there."
"Where's the jack? Jack her up, will you?"
"Yeah, yeah, yeah."
"You get that fresh rubber?"
"Got it."
"Maybe that'll make the bastard go."
"Yeah, yeah, yeah."

The track opens for qualification runs at noon. Clouds are piling up overhead, the sky over the track is the color of ashes. Anybody who hasn't qualified better get out there and run. The qualified men are doing their rain dances. Should rain fall, there will be no rain date. The field will go as it stands. Bumped from the race yesterday, Tom Bigelow surges noisily onto the track in a backup car in a desperate effort to get back in.

141

The transistor radio in garage number 12 is tuned in to the broadcast of the time trials. Reception could be better, static crackling like popcorn on a stove. The doors to the garage are ajar, crossed by a string of small checkered flags wound around two garbage drums to keep stray people from bumbling in. Number 42 squats in the middle of the garage. Don Mergard, the owner, a good-looking man, his big face loose and pouchy, is tramping up and down like a wounded animal. A blue driver's uniform dangles from a hook on the wall, looking like the skeleton of a man who hanged himself. A crewman is skimming a newspaper, resting inert on his knees. Another crewman is settled on a box, peering glassy-eyed into space, like a hesitant mourner. The mood is awful. They are, as it is said, "hanging the crepe." This is the garage of Jan Opperman, the man on the bubble. A re-tired businessman, Mergard has never been to Indian-apolis before. He trundled in from Cincinnati, with one car, one engine, no spare parts. Opperman put a minimal number of practice laps on the car, knowing that if any-thing broke there would be no parts to replace it. He borrowed bits and pieces from other cars, wheeling and dealing his way to speed. A suspension part here. A wheel there. A brace here. A good portion of Gasoline Alley contributed to Opperman's racer. Not the way to do Indianapolis. Yet, as of now, the car is in the race. Opper-man, at the moment, is lounging on the grass in the first turn, escorting around some friends. No spectators mill outside the garage where Mergard paces.

"Well, this is racing," Mergard says, his voice little more than a hoarse whisper.

"Yeah, well Don, you made the only decision there was to make. The long-range forecast was rain this weekend. The guys who qualified yesterday ran five miles an hour faster than they practiced. They ran on a cool day. We ran on a hot day."

"We should have been in."

"We were running consistently three miles an hour

faster than these guys. Makes you wonder sometimes about the clocks."

"Damn, we should have been in the field."

"We could have run 183 or 184 yesterday."

"That's big-time auto racing."

"A matter of luck. That's what it all comes down to, a matter of luck."

"Sometimes you get the feeling, what's the use of it all, this life."

The radio: "And the green is out. And Bigelow is on it . . ."

One of the crewmen begins to gnaw his nails. Mergard drops into a chair, clasps his hands under his chin. They feel their mood declining.

"Tom Bigelow drives into that first turn, very nicely into one, left-side tires right on the line . . . off the first corner into the short chute, a very nice line . . . down the straightaway, about two feet from the wall . . . tools down the straight as he tries to bump his way back into the Indianapolis 500 of 1976 . . . up to top speed, he enters turn number three a little high, comes down onto the line . . . comes out of the fourth turn very smoothly, checks with his crew, and comes down to complete the first lap of his qualifying run."

Mergard gets up and paces again. He strokes the stubble on his chin.

"Tom Bigelow again very nicely through one, up close to the wall in the short chute, into the second turn. Again, both wheels on the left side just touching the line at one point . . . off two, down into the backstretch . . . seems to be running very smoothly . . . and it is plenty good enough to move into the starting lineup . . . 49.32 seconds. Speed— 182.482. Tom Bigelow should be a happy man today."

"There we go," Mergard says.

"Cincinnati, here we come."

With a mile an hour to spare, Bigelow requalifies for the race. Rolled in to be interviewed, he credits his crew, the car, his owner, his sponsor.

Praise of a detergent pours out of the radio. One of the crewmen shuffles out of the garage, slides onto a small bicycle, and says, "Think I'll go lose myself."

Mergard scoops up the abandoned paper and gazes at it without seeing words.

The other crewman says, "It sure hurts when you run for a million dollars."

Cross-legged in the first turn, Opperman is thinking to himself, "Boy, I wish I had another ride to get into. I wish I had gone faster. I wish I had gone just a couple of miles an hour faster." Pushing himself up, he stumbles back to Gasoline Alley, dejected. When he arrives there, he bumps into Mergard trudging out of the garage, hands dug deep into his pockets.

"What a bummer," Opperman says.

"Yeah," Mergard says.

"You going back today?"

"Maybe later."

"I should talk to you before you go."

"Okay. We can all get together and lock up the garage."

Opperman shuffles past. "What're you gonna do?" someone asks.

"I'm just waiting for the Lord to direct me," he says.

Last night, feeling sure he would be bumped today, Opperman phoned his wife, Mary Lou, in Montana. "You call your lady when you're feeling pretty bad. She's got her head wired on." Later on, his wife called back. After she hung up, she said she phoned a friend and told her what was going on. The woman said she would pray for Jan. She called back and said God had given her a prophecy that Jan was not going to be eliminated from the field. Calm down. Opperman was feeling better. He hung up and phoned a friend in Florida. Without Opperman mentioning his wife's call, the friend told Opperman he, too, had had a prophecy, and it revealed that Opperman would be in the race. Opperman was feeling much better. He figured it was going to rain. Out of the race

144

and no sign of another car, Opperman is now wondering about the Father.

A lull in qualifying. The sun has broken through, but there is a breeze. Some of the racing men in the pits say they figure a number of drivers are waiting for the wind to die down. It doesn't seem like much of a wind, but when you figure speed to three decimal points, even a breeze counts. Or they are waiting till the air cools later in the day. Or they are playing possum, not caring to make their runs till they know exactly what they have to beat. There is no end of theories and analyses to listen to.

During the lull, the track is opened for practice. A number of cars throb onto the course. Soon Johnny Parsons comes out to continue his reliability check. Chassis adjustments have been made on the car. The engine coughs, catches, rackets, jittery with power, and Parsons growls onto the track. The speeds of drivers "knocking on the door" are shouted out over the public address system. Lloyd Ruby—183. Lee Kunzman—179. Mike Hiss—178.

Listening to the speeds, Tassi Vatis says, "It's gonna be one hectic afternoon. One thing for sure, I'm glad we're not in on it." Vatis has been through such afternoons before. So has Parsons.

Parsons turns a series of laps in the low 180s. Then Lloyd Ruby's car is put in line for a qualifying run, and the track is shut down. Parsons coasts in. Bill Finley and John Barnes crowd around, and Parsons begins pouring out information.

"It's pushing a little," he says. "The engine feels strong. The gauges were all okay. Just that little push."

"Okay, check the stagger," Finley says.

"Stagger okay."

"Let's take her back. We've run enough."

Roughly a hundred and twenty-five miles have been put on the car in the last three days, and the engine has held up. The plan is to take the engine out now, then put the first engine back in for the race, once it's rebuilt.

"What do you think?" someone asks Barnes.

"We're as confident as you can be in this business."

Lloyd Ruby clicks off four timed laps and knocks Bobby Olivero out of the field. All week, everyone has been reassuring Olivero that his speed was safe. No one could touch him. There weren't enough fast cars left. Don't worry. He had worried. After Ruby finishes his run, Olivero kneels down outside his garage, covers his face with his hands, and weeps.

"All the guys do it," says a driver watching nearby. "It hurts. You can't express the hurt. This race can tear your heart out."

Janet Guthrie announces she won't try to qualify— her car is too slow. There will be no women in the race.

With a little over two hours of qualifying time remaining, David Hobbs bounds out on his third and final attempt. Yesterday, Hobbs's car would run only 177 miles per hour. His twelve-man crew worked in shifts of four through the night to rebuild the engine in hopes of pumping up the power. Averaging over 183 miles per hour, Hobbs handily makes the field. He bumps Bill Simpson. Simpson is the head of Simpson Safety Equipment Corporation, which turns out the seat belts and driver's uniform that Hobbs just used in bumping Simpson.

As the track reopens for practice, drama begins to unfold along the pit apron. Jerry Karl, a middling driver, is turning practice laps in car number 8, the Routh Meat Packing Special. They are too slow. Wearing street clothes, Jan Opperman is strolling down the pit apron, feeling sure he is going to get a ride somewhere, somehow. A man motions him over to the wall.

"Hey," he says. "I just wanted to tell you I really like the things you're doing and that you stand for. I really think you're together. I've been into some heavy praying myself lately, and it's improved my life."

146

"That's great," Opperman says.

They talk on for a while.

"By the way," the man says. "My name is Dick Routh."

"Routh?" Opperman says, a thought clicking in his head. "Hey, do you own that car there?"

"Yeah, I do."

"Well, see, I have this driver's uniform back in the garage."

Ten minutes after five, Opperman drones out onto the track, the third man to sit in car number 8. Opperman assured Routh he could run faster than Jerry Karl. He has no idea how. Routh, however, is desperate. The gambling instinct runs strong in the blood of owners of unqualified cars. They begin to use their cars as they would high stakes on a gaming table, playing them on the racetrack according to hunch and hope.

Opperman turns a few laps around 175 miles per hour and comes in.

"The car's loose. It's wiggling out there."

Adjustments are made, and Opperman blurts back out. Meanwhile, the crew scurries to the garage to get fresh tires on which to make a qualifying attempt.

"Come on, get ready to go in line," shouts Todd Gibson, the chief mechanic. There is fright in his eyes.

Opperman runs some laps in the high 178s, then pulls in. Tires are changed.

"The car is wiggling down pit lane," Opperman says.

"Just go fast enough to qualify and that's all," Gibson says.

Opperman looks at him, seems to be searching for the proper words. "I hope I can go that fast."

"Somebody get down there and tell them we want to go."

"We'll be down there."

Opperman tells Gibson he wants to put some wear on the new tires, "scuff them in," before he makes his run. But wait. His crew suddenly realizes there isn't enough fuel in the tank to complete four laps. At 5:25 the crew

147

moves like men in a panic as it hurries the car back to the garage. It's immediately put in line. A Goodyear engineer toddles over.

"The new tires will mean a mile and a half," he says.

"Yeah?" Opperman says, lifting his brows.

The car is shoved down near the starting line. Opperman buckles himself in and is given the qualifying instructions.

"What do I need?"

"180.7."

"Brother."

"Wind her up."

At 5:39 Opperman storms onto the track. More cars are being parked in the qualification line. If a man's got something with four wheels and an engine, it's time to put it in line. Opperman does three warmup laps and doesn't take the green flag.

"She's pushing bad," he says. "If I had stayed out there, I would have run into the fence. I definitely would have run into the fence."

"Let's check the stagger."

"Yeah, the stagger's gone."

"The stagger went off, Jan."

A crewman stoops down by the rear tires. Two pounds of air hiss out of the left rear, two pounds hiss into the right rear. Three cars sit stacked up in front of Opperman. Seventeen minutes of qualifying time remain, normally enough to handle three attempts. Many drivers and mechanics have gathered out on the line to stand watch over the last-minute madness, relieved no end that they are merely spectators.

A pair of crewmen from qualified cars stare at the rear of Opperman's racer and frown. "Look at that," one of them says. "Hell, there's no way in the world that'll be in this race. Might as well park it right now."

Bent-headed, solemn, Opperman sits helmetless in the race car. His hands are clasped in front of him. He swallows several quarts of air. "I kept wishing all these people who were telling me I wasn't going to make the show would leave me alone. I was involved in pretty serious prayer. I was asking for some help because I knew I needed it. I was saying that if I belong in this race, let me drive with every bit of ability I've got."

At 5:46 Mike Hiss pulls off the track after taking two warmup laps, not able to generate enough speed. Mel Kenyon's car is fired up.

"Boy, it's gonna be close," Todd Gibson says.

"We're tight," Opperman says.

Kenyon takes the green after one warmup lap. He runs under 180 his first lap and the crew flags him in. Eight minutes. The car of rookie Billy Engelhart is started. The engine stalls. It catches the second time. If Opperman is on the course at six o'clock, his run will count. He is shoved to the starting line for the third time, the second time in sixteen minutes. He knows the instructions by heart. He straps his helmet on as Engelhart, in the hairpiece special, whirls by on his first warmup lap. Behind Opperman in line is Jim McElreath. McElreath has his helmet on and is sitting in his car. Behind him Mike Hiss is standing next to his car, expressionless, a lick of brown hair coming down over one eyebrow. He knows it is over. Behind him Mel Kenyon is buckled in his car and has his helmet on. Kenyon must be the most optimistic man in all of Indianapolis. His odds of getting on the track are roughly several trillion to one.

Engelhart turns a lap at 177.7 miles per hour, much too slow, and his crew ushers him in. Number 8 is fired up, churning to life with a throaty roar. With less than a minute left, Opperman is given the signal to move out. As he sweeps through turn one after completing one warmup lap, the gun sounds. Opperman still has to somehow find three miles an hour. He takes the green the second time past.

The man on the bubble, Eldon Rasmussen, no longer in his driver's uniform, is standing at the starting line, where he has been for the last hour, counting off the minutes. He is tight-lipped. It is as if six o'clock is a guillotine, and his neck is on the block. "I'm sure Opperman won't make it," Rasmussen tells himself. "He just hasn't been going fast enough. It would be incredible, just unbelievable, if he made it. He just can't do it."

From the loudspeakers: "Jan Opperman into the first turn, down onto the white line with both left-side wheels, into the short chute . . . Jan Opperman, the last qualifier for 1976, heading down the backstretch, gets down almost two car widths off the wall . . . Jan Opperman. Car number 8. Maybe ten or twelve hot laps so far in this car today . . . into the third turn very smoothly, just down to the line, out close to the wall as he goes through the short chute . . . comes out of the fourth corner . . . Jan Opperman, arriving in the mainstretch to complete the first lap of his qualifying attempt."

The roar as he thunders past. Stopwatches are consulted.

"Stays above the white line as he goes through one this time, about two feet off the wall as he goes through the short chute into the second turn, down to the white line . . . comes off, exits very smoothly, close to the wall, about two car widths off the wall as he comes down the backstretch . . . herrrrrree's the speed. And it is fast enough for Jan Opperman—49.66 seconds. Speed—181.232 for Jan Opperman." A great roar of joy goes up from the big crowd. Opperman, out on the track, the last man to race against the clock, is accomplishing the impossible.

"I can't believe it," Rasmussen is thinking. "Holy shit. I can't believe this is happening to me."

The applause keeps up. So does Opperman. He runs a faster lap. Another. One additional lap, and the last man enters the field for the sixtieth running of the race. Rasmussen is bumped. Starting the day in thirty-third position in number 42, Jan Opperman finishes in number 8. He will start the race thirty-third and last.

Welcomed by big cheers, Opperman glides into the pits, his crew hysterically mobbing him. They pound his helmet before he can crawl out of the racer. He is rubbed, patted, squeezed, kneaded. "My Father in heaven took care of that ride," Opperman says.

"That was a little closer than you wanted it, wasn't it, Jan?"

"Well, that's the way my Father does things, to keep me from being a spoiled kid. If I got everything I wanted, I'd get out of hand."

Bulbs flash. Opperman's small daughter trots over and embraces him. Then he walks over to the fence cutting off the grandstands from the pits. A comely blonde, Opperman's wife, rushes over and hugs him hard. "You made it," she says. "You made it." Tears well in her eyes.

The racetrack empties. Crews in the garages are chugging beer and chatting softly. Indianapolis is cautiously darkening. Street sounds blend in a soft hollow note, as if someone has stopped playing but has still kept his foot on the piano pedal. First to last, the difference in total time among the thirty-three cars qualified for the Indianapolis 500 is seven and fifty-nine hundredths seconds. Eldon Rasmussen, the first alternate, missed the race by fifty-one hundredths of a second.

★★★★★★★★★★★★★★★★

The hurry-scurry, the angry hum of recent weeks has departed. A quivering stillness descends. Gasoline Alley enters a different mood. The race is near and the final work has begun. The track will not open till Thursday, when one last practice session will be held. There is a somnolent air as the flat tedium goes on. The place has the personality of a gargantuan army barracks. Bill Finley picks away at the chassis of number 93, minus its engine. John Barnes is fiddling with the gearbox. Music falls from the stereo, reporting on a junk-food junkie. "This is when the real work begins," Finley snorts. "This is work week."

"Do you think we can still get more speed out of this car?" Barnes asks.

Finley says, "The best way to find the top speed of this car is to find a mine shaft. She won't run any faster than straight down."

Finley has a hankering for practical jokes, finding delight in seeing others with egg on their face. There was the time Bobby Unser had rented a car. He made the mistake of mentioning to Finley that, with rental cars looking so alike, he wondered how he was ever going to find his car in the parking lot. Finley knew how. He painted black X's all over the car. Unser found it. There was the time Finley decided to pay a visit to Dan Gurney, a car owner who lives on the West Coast. He drove over to Gurney's home with a pickup truck brimming with trash. He dumped the trash on Gurney's front lawn and roared on his way.

Hoyt Brewer, a hollow-eyed machinist at the Allison engine factory, is scrubbing parts in a sink, the enamel eaten away. The faucet sputters softly. Very gently, he douses the parts under the water, working grime free with his fingers. Brewer is one of the rag-tag crew members who uses his vacation time, for no money, to work on Parsons' car. "I do it just for the heck of it. I do any damn thing they tell me to do. Clean parts. Run errands. Mop up the floor. Wipe the car. Somebody's got to do the dirty work. Might as well be me."

Shorty Harrison is chewing on a bologna sandwich. He cradles a can of beer in his other hand. He normally works on the assembly line at Bryant Heating and Cooling. "The job of every member of the pit crew is to be a soldier, ready for anything. One day you might be asked to change tires, another day to push the car to the fueling area, and the day after to sweep the floor. You're a baby-sitter to the car. You feed it, give it enemas, take it out for a walk."

Throughout the alley, jittery crews are tearing engines and chassis apart, searching yet again for problems they pray aren't there. The crewmen joust with each other and now and then look at their watches. Men from unqualified cars packing to leave stop by for a wistful last look. Parts that receive a lot of stress are being carted in boxes to Magnaflux stations downtown, where they are x-rayed, the way airplane parts are, to locate invisible points of weakness, hairline fissures, before the parts fail on the track and send the car careening off the road at 200 miles an hour. Every time a critical part is replaced on a car, it is first Magnafluxed. For days, the race machines will sit like skeletons—parts here, parts there—then gradually they will be reassembled for the last time. Drivers, meanwhile, with no cars to run, will worry. There is much to worry about the last week before the race.

Few people outside of crewmen hang around in the garages, and most of those are from among the four thousand four hundred reporters and cameramen who cover the race, tracking down one more interview, questioning anyone who has a mouth. Along the pit apron, painters are brushing the names of cars and drivers on the low inside pit wall to signify where each car will pit during the race. Pits are assigned according to qualifying speeds, the faster cars sitting down near the first corner. Large parts are being hosed outside the garages with high-pressure water jets, like garden sprays, spurting water with the same eccentric motion but faster, flinging lumps of water with almost the speed of a bullet to clean out debris from every surface and crevice.

Four crew members from A. J. Foyt's team are shooting craps outside Foyt's garage. Foyt is looking on. A barrel-chested man scoops up the dice and jumbles them in his hands.

"Boy," Foyt says. "If somebody picked up dice like that I'd put him on my knee and slap him."

"C'mon six," the crewman urges as the dice are in the air. "Let's see a little six."

Four.

He tosses the dice again.

"C'mon little six. Lemme see six."

Four.

"Little six, little six. C'mon little six. Why can't I see you, six?"

Craps.

Ticket sales are going better than ever. A record crowd seems in store. Fran Derr, the head of the ticket department, presents a matronly appearance; her face is clever and energetic. In her sixties, she has run the ticket department for twenty-five years. She is famous for her efficiency. Although she has no trouble remembering people's names, Derr tends more often to match people with where they sit. She sees the seat beneath the face. Most ticket buyers come year after year, and they like as not keep the same seats, and thus somebody will walk into the Speedway office and Derr will think, "Yes, I remember you. You're Tower Terrace, Section D." Tickets go for five dollars to fifty dollars, and no matter what you pay, you can't see more than a third of the course. Once you've bought a seat, you have first priority on it for the following year. The most popular seats are Paddock Sections A, B, and E, which cradle the stretch of straightaway that runs down past the starting line into the first turn, and the Tower Terrace seats, which rise behind the pits. The turnover in these seats is less than 1 percent. "I do all I can to keep the names of these seat holders secret," Derr says. "This helps keep down the homicide rate."

Every time a new stand goes up at the track, and one goes up almost every year, Derr makes it her business to go out and try it out from various vantage points. She sits there, imagining cars and watching air. In her mind, she registers what portions of the course are plainly visible, whether any of the harried pit action can be caught, whether the scoreboards are in view. If she were going to watch the race, Derr would settle herself in the Vista stand on the first turn, where she could see the cars whistling down the long straight, sliding through the first turn, gunning down the short chute. As it is, Derr sees as much as is visible from the inside of the Speedway office. She saw the race once, on her first trip to the track back in 1933. Then a nineteen-year-old nursing student, she arrived with some college friends without tickets. A man sought them out and told them that the race was sold out. It happened, though, that he had some tickets. Twenty dollars a seat. They paid. Pushing through the gates, they learned that inside the ticket office, piles of seats were still being sold. They were selling for a dollar apiece.

Ever since she came to work as ticket chief, Derr

155

has made her life one long battle against ticket scalpers. Her consuming objective is to run all the scalpers out of town. "I can easily sum up my feelings about scalpers," she says. "I abhor them. They are a menace to the human race. I'll fight them till the day I die, and after that I'll return and haunt them." By various methods she declines to discuss, Derr has already done in a great many scalpers, and she feels a certain sense of satisfaction that the problem appears to have moderated. She derives particular pleasure out of watching a scalper, hours before the race, trying frantically to unload his tickets for less than he paid for them.

Derr does her best to guard the identity of the Indianapolis block buyers, the companies and organizations that gobble up large chunks of tickets. Some block buyers grab thousands of seats. Were the names to get out, Derr is sure throngs of fans would harass them for seats. Her personal favorite among the blocks is a group of Australians who have been coming for ten years. They have one complaint: they don't like the taste of American beer.

Tonight another party is on tap, this time to honor the three men beginning the race from the last row— David Hobbs, Tom Bigelow, and Jan Opperman. Bigelow, as it happens, doesn't show up. It is a light affair, put on at the Indianapolis Press Club. Featured on the menu are three sandwiches: the David Hobbs Sandwich—lean country ham on rye; the Tom Bigelow Sandwich—peppered meat loaf on bun; the Jan Opperman Bumper Special—shrimpburger on bun. Most people seem to be going for the Hobbs ham. The printed program for the evening is stuffed with oddball last row facts: fourteen winners of the race at one time sat in the back row. Two last-placers both started and finished in last place. A prince—Prince de Cystria—ingloriously qualified for the last row in 1923. Same for David Bruce-Brown, in 1911 and 1912, perhaps because his mother used to trail him around the country in her private railroad car, telling everyone who would listen what an idiot her son was. The Last Row Hall of Fame is listed, requiring three appearances in the back row for membership. Eight men belong, the most notable being Bill Cheesbourg, who started dead last in 1958, 1964, and 1965.

The emcee gets up and says, "The ones who once sat with us. Two years ago, inspired by the many words of encouragement he received here, Bob Harkey started thirty-first and soared to eighth place. Did success spoil Bob Harkey? Yep, it sure did. This year, he's in the tenth row."

Opperman cuts a swath through the tables and strides up to the podium, where he is presented with a check for thirty-three cents. "Ain't gonna do much, but I'll take it," he says. "I'm real tickled to be in the show. I know old Rasmussen ain't too tickled. . . . I hope I race good and hard and represent to the world a good racer, because I feel like I'm representing you folks. I'll be standing on the pedal for you. I don't hope to finish where I'm starting."

Hobbs speaks to the assemblage. He receives a check for thirty-one cents. Hobbs comes from Upper Boddington, England. "People always want to know, if there's an Upper Boddington, is there a Lower Boddington?" he says. "There most certainly is a Lower Boddington, and with money like this, I might have to go and live there. This ain't gonna do much for the bank account." Lots of laughter. More talk. More drinking. People drift out. Time to go.

★★★★★★★★★★★★★★★★

The Speedway Bar isn't much. Ruthlessly up-to-date. Bar stools fitted with seat belts. Walls of featureless gold wallpaper, oil paintings of race cars. The ceiling is beige. The chairs are rust-colored imitation leather with chrome-tubing legs. There is a long wooden bar, lit murkily in muted shades of red and blue. Around fifteen tables. Nice-looking waitresses in black and white outfits. They have the appearance of walking checkered flags. A sign on the cash register behind the bar reads: RESPECT YOUR BARTENDER. Parked against the back wall is an upright piano, necklaced by a smaller bar. Wanda, a blowsy woman with sulfur hair pulled back in a bun, is belting out songs that led the charts in 1940. By eight-thirty the place is jammed.

The dance floor is moving with easy action; lovers are purring at linoleum tables in the corner. Crewmen finished with their labors, drivers, race experts, hustlers, operators, and plain fans mingle with each other. Jeans, bush jackets, and three-piece suits pass through the bar. Amid the free flow of expensive whiskey, a squab-nosed man wearing a greasy T-shirt booms up to the bar and yells to nobody in particular, "Goddamned. What day is this—Tuesday, Wednesday? What the hell day is it?"

"Wednesday. It's Wednesday," someone answers.

158

"That's right," he babbles. "You know, this year when I was home out in Seattle, I says to the wife, 'Listen, I'm goin' to Indy again,' she gives me a lot of flack about it. Ranting and raving, ready to throw the good china. So I started knocking her around till I drill some common sense into her meatball. Been coming here twelve years, so why stop? Ain't nothin' gonna keep me away from this joint. I love to see these brutes. This is the magic moment in sport. Nothin' like it."

He laughs. "Hell, yes," he continues. "People asked where I was going and I said, 'Indy, to the Indy 500.' And there would be envy in their eyes. I saw it. So here I am. Maybe it was some goddamn drive, but soon as I remember, by God, I was here for the Indy 500, man that's all I need to know. I tell you, it's delightful, just delightful to be here. Who gives a damn who wins or loses. It's just delightful to be here with you folks. . . ."

A thin man with a pencil moustache is hunkered over a Scotch beside a gravel-faced man with eyes set in deep wells.

"You see how fast those things go?"

"I know it."

"Somethin' isn't it?"

"Those guys are as good as dead if something happens. They've bought an acre." He sips his beer.

"I wonder how they feel about that. How do they feel?"

"Ask one. Go ahead, ask one. They'll talk to you. If they're not real busy, they'll talk to you."

"Yeah?" He squints as if solving a problem.

"It takes a while to get used to looking at these guys. You think they're supermen. It takes, oh, maybe two or three years until you get really used to looking at them. I've done it, so I'm used to them. I used to foam at the mouth and all at first. You'll change too, you'll see."

"Maybe I'll give it a try."

A knot of angry men lean against the wall, jawing.

"This is a show here, boy, ain't it?"

"More a show than a race."

"Gotta think A. J., big ole A. J., will take it."

"He'll be on the pedal. I know he'll be on the pedal."

"Wasn't expecting him to be on the brake."

A man has been mooning over one of the waitresses for over an hour.

"You know, I knew a guy once who bought a pregnant elephant."

"Oh, yeah?" says the waitress.

"He figured he'd make a killing. Two for the price of one. Make a real killing."

"Sounds like a good idea." She smiles dimly.

"Do you know how long it takes for an elephant to have a baby?"

"No, how long?" Her eyes narrow.

"Two or three years."

"Wow!" She nods gravely.

"He was hit with boarding and feeding that damned thing for a couple of years. It wiped him out. He finally gave the blasted thing away."

A potbellied man in jeans comes in. He wobbles a bit, but he is grinning.

"Sam, you bastard, get the hell in here," calls a man from the bar.

"Hey, Larry," says the chubby man.

"Sit down before you fall on your face."

"Buy me a drink, ya pizza face."

"Your ass I will."

He glances over at one of the waitresses. "You look tired."

"I am," she says.

"Why don't you come on back to my room, and I'll charge your battery."

"Will you look at my differential while you're at it?"

★★★★★★★★★★★★★★★

The last day the big race cars can practice is called Carburetion Day, now a misnomer. At first, the purpose was to allow the cars to test their carburetion systems. Carburetors haven't been used on Indianapolis cars for twenty-five years. All the machines are fuel-injected. Still, the day is important. For two reasons: to make sure a newly rebuilt engine is all right, and to find out fuel mileage. There is a fuel limit for the race—two hundred and eighty gallons. The brutish power of the engines must be harnessed to give enough mileage to go the distance; cars can run out. Once the last dribble of fuel is gone, there is nothing to do but coast.

The day is clear and warm. Suntan day. Before very long in the three-hour practice period, thirty-two of the thirty-three starters put in an appearance on the asphalt. The roar of the engines begins to build up like the roll of a huge kettledrum. The first alternate also blurts out for some laps. The second alternate is not here; he has already left for home. History says he should. Only twice in the fifty-nine years of the race has an alternate sneaked into the field. In 1914, one of the qualifiers demolished his car in practice and allowed the first alternate to start the race. In 1929, a starter took his car out of the lineup because it was vibrating badly. The first alternate, at this late stage, had left. The second alternate completed the field. He probably wished he had left, too. He got involved in a wicked accident that wiped out his car. Of this year's starting field, the only driver not on the track is Johnny Parsons. His new engine isn't done. The crew is vexed.

"We should be out there," Bill Finley says. "You should put some laps on a new motor before the race. Usually, every car is out there. I was up till four o'clock in the morning before I just gave up. That engine ought to be done." Finley strides along out to the pits, thumbs hooked in his pants pockets, bent forward as if bucking a strong wind.

Alongside him, Parsons says, "I'm disappointed. If there are any small bugs to work out, we could have solved them. I guess mostly it's a psychological disadvantage, not being out there and knowing for sure everything's all right. It didn't happen to anyone else."

A big crowd has trooped out to watch the final laps. Good speeds are being registered. Rutherford—187.931. Andretti—187.266. Foyt—186.451. Al Unser—183.861. Surprisingly, the fastest lap of all is turned in by Tom Sneva at 188.166. Much to think about on who will win this race. Mechanics are carefully poring over engines, knowing that fresh engines can be duds. They show up from time to time. The vulnerability of a modern, ultra-sophisticated race car, despite its huge cost, is great. The beating it takes at the speed and distance it runs is considerable. It is no comfort to know that a car has run hundreds of miles without a single mishap. On the contrary, the longer engines last the more mechanics keep knocking wood.

Krisiloff barrels out in the backup car and musters a number of laps above 180. There appear to be no worries with the car. In jeans and a short-sleeved shirt, Parsons is settled on the pit wall, watching the mechanics jimmy with Krisiloff's car, while he drains a can of Gatorade. He drinks in quick gulps and then mops his mouth with his handkerchief, imitating a man with a big moustache who has just chugged a glass of foamy beer.

A crewman from another racer wanders by. "Hey, why ain't ya out there, Johnny?"

Parsons makes a face. "Ah, I don't need any practice. I don't like to wear myself out for nothing." He sniggers.

"Sure. Sure," the crewman grins.

"You'll see on race day."

Yesterday morning, Jimmy "the Greek" came out with his odds for the race. He's got Johnny Rutherford and A. J. Foyt at four-to-one. Al Unser and Gordon Johncock are six-to-one. Pancho Carter and Tom Sneva are eight-to-one. Andretti is ten-to-one. The local papers have odds of their own. Foyt, Rutherford, and Al Unser are four-to-one. Mario Andretti is six-to-one. Bobby Unser and Johncock are seven-to-one. Parsons is eleven-to-one, the twelfth favorite to take the race.

After practice wraps up, the crews are allowed an hour of pit drill with the car engines killed. Seven to twelve times during the five hundred miles, a car will have to stop in the pits to get fuel, to get fresh rubber. A driver may try to make more stops if there are yellow flags. Under the yellow, the field moves slowly, and not as much time is lost from pit stops. As tireless as factory workers, the men who do the fueling and change the tires figure importantly in the race. Outcomes are sometimes decided along the pit apron.

Using the backup car, the Parsons crew gets going with its drills, wearing matching pink and white uniforms. Finley is supervising. His trousers are spotted and rumpled, his hair shooting every which way. He needs a shave. A reporter is wedged into the driver's seat for the practice, and the crew yanks the car back a few hundred feet and then shoves it forward. A pit crew that is fast and seasoned is a sight to behold. Standing behind the pit wall, Shorty thrusts out a long pole with a stop sign welded to it to show the driver where to brake. "Not much technique to it. You just put it out." Only five men are permitted over the wall during a stop, though any number may be in the pit. Two tire men and the jack man are already over the wall as the car screeches to a stop. Texas shoves a quick-action platform jack underneath that hoists the right side of the car off the ground in one swift motion, while Mike Herion stoops down and starts to change the right-front tire and John Barnes does the same with the right-rear tire. Normally, only the two right tires are changed; they get all the hard wear, since the cars turn only left on the track and thus lean to the right. Though they rarely wear out, the tires are switched because cooler rubber affords better adhesion; so tires are changed, allowed to cool off, and then slapped back on later in the race. The wheels are attached with large lug nuts. The device that gets them off is a Black & Decker Air Impact Wrench, connected by hose to a big tank of nitrogen, capable of spinning a nut off in a few seconds. The nuts are fastened to the wheels by springs, so when they are spun off, they remain attached to the wheel. This way the tire men don't have to touch them—during the race they are hot enough to melt a finger. "Skeee-reeet-skeee-reet-skeereeet" go the air wrenches, carrying above all other sounds. Off spin the nuts. Off come the old wheels. On goes new rubber. "Skee-reet-skee-reet." Meanwhile, Matt Murphy stuffs a round hose into the fuel opening on the side of the car. Pressurized hoses aren't allowed, so the fuel is stored in tanks atop tall stilts, like long-legged bugs, to speed the gravity flow. Working alongside Murphy is Reny Filiatreau, a quiet and benevolent man who heads the service department of a local Chevrolet dealer and is Bill Finley's next-door neighbor. He shoves a hose connected to an upside-down milk bottle into a second opening known as the vent. This frees trapped air from the tank, while telling him when the tank is full. When fuel bubbles into the hose, the tank has all it can take. If Parsons is thirsty, a crewman will pass him a drink in a cup set in a metal ring attached to a long pole. Some drivers also want chewing gum; Foyt, for instance, cannot race without fresh spearmint. The gas man finishes, and the jack man yanks the jack from beneath the car. The stop takes nineteen seconds.

Hunching his shoulders, Finley says, "I figure it takes about fourteen seconds to fill a tank, so if we can do the tires in fourteen, that would be a minimum stop."

"Yup, that sounds right," Barnes says.

"Jack man," Finley says, "after the car's up, plant your foot over the end of the jack so the jack don't accidentally slip off. That could be a mess."

Texas nods.

"When you change those tires, Mike, make sure the tire you take off is flat on the ground before the fresh one goes on. If it bounces just once, it's gone. It'll roll all the way down the pits. You got six pins to fit over the wheel to be snug. Stay out there three days if you have to, but make damn sure those pins are in. If the pins stick, just use your air wrench like a mallet and beat that son of a bitch until she's on."

Finley turns to Reny. "The minute you see fuel spit into the tube, pull it out. Pull it the hell out. Leave it in a second longer, it'll be full. Then you've got to cradle the vent like she's a baby doll and take it to the tank and empty the fuel in. We need every drop."

During the race, Robin Miller, a sportswriter with the *Indianapolis Star,* will serve as the board man. Positioned a shade off the racing macadam with a giant slateboard, he will be the link between Parsons and the crew. On the board, he will scribble information in big letters— Parsons' position in the race, the lap number, when he should pull in—then he will hold the slate aloft so Parsons can see it as he whistles by. For his own safety, Miller is forbidden by racing rules to leave his post once the race starts; if he does, he faces a five-hundred-dollar fine. Meanwhile, in the pits, Tassi Vatis will monitor the fuel mileage by reading a slender tube attached to the fuel tank striped with markings that tell how much is gone. Mike Griffin, a local record producer, will be the scorer. Using a Lab-Chrom electronic timer and charts, he will scratch down the total elapsed time every lap Parsons passes by, keeping his pit stops also, to run a check against the official scorers for the race.

Finley takes some practice now on the right-front tire, which he will change in the race, allowing Mike Herion to work the front on the backup car. Finley says, "Now who's gonna carry me over the wall when I'm done?"

Barnes says, "Just hold on to the hose and we'll rope you in."

"Sounds good."

During the drill, the jack is allowed to drop before the tires are firmly on the car. Finley gives a spitball of a glance. "When you set that car down, you got to be goddamn sure there's tires on it. Soon as it's down, the driver's gonna take off."

Changing tires and pumping in fuel goes on. It is tense, hard work, and the pitmen get numbed to where the heat and the exertion don't bother them. The men seem to loosen and quicken their pace as they get deeper into work; breaks between stops grow longer and more frequent. They sit on the concrete wall to the side of the car passing dripping ice-chest Cokes and Gatorades Vatis has provided, gazing over at the race car and the spare tires stacked next to it.

"Must be total concentration," Finley says. "Total concentration. We need fourteen-seconders. None of this dillying around. We ain't got time to burn out here."

"Ah, Finley," Shorty says. "Parsons'll be so far out front he'll be able to stop for lunch."

Finley says, "If he's that far ahead, I'll broil him a steak and cut it for him too."

The afternoon wears on in skee-reets and clanks. The times improve—16.8 seconds, 14.7 seconds, 14.8 seconds.

Parsons comes out to watch and runs through the signals he will use on the track to pass gobbets of information to the crew. Twisting his wrist outward means the car is running loose. Motioning his fingers to the right means it's pushing. Pointing backward over his head means there's engine trouble. Pointing straight behind asks who's running next in position, pointing forward asks who's in front of him. Raising one finger, he wants the right-rear tire changed, two fingers for both right-side tires, three for the left-front as well, and four for new tires all around. Thumping on his helmet means he needs a relief driver. When signaling, Parsons must be careful not to lift his arm much above the steering wheel. At 200 miles per hour, if he raised his arm above the windshield, the tremendous pressure of the wind would rip his arm out of its socket. It has happened.

The practice period over, the crew scuffs back with the car to the garage. A mechanic passing by says, "How's it going, boys?"

Finley says, "Well, we got the race in our back pocket, maybe you heard. Now we're just biding time till we pull into Victory Lane."

"You know the way?"

"Run two hundred laps and average 180 miles an hour."

★★★★★★★★★★★★★★★★

The drivers are trundling into place for the driver's prerace meeting. Out in the pit area, a stone's throw from the starting line, a makeshift bleacher has been tossed up, three creaky rows high, with folding chairs arranged neatly along the rows. The men slide into their seats, placing themselves in the same order in which they will begin the race. They shuffle and stuff their hands in their pockets, waiting for the meeting to get started. Some lay back in their seats, sweating in the humid morning air, while others rock slowly and some clown with each other. There are nods and hellos from the men already seated, car and woman and weather conversations to drift into, and crowd noise coming from all sides.

One by one, the drivers are introduced to the crowd, maybe ten thousand or so, and as their names are called they flash a smile and offer a small wave. A variety of awards are given out, trophies and cash and checks, celebrities are brought out, and then chief steward Tom Binford rises and takes the microphone. He stands erect before the drivers and gives out a narrow grin.

"Now, gentlemen, we've had meetings before, and

we've had some memos out, and what I'm going to try to do right now is to highlight some of the things we'd like you to keep in mind between now and the time the race is over tomorrow." He pauses. "First, let me remind you about the pit entrance. Make sure you stay to the left of the broken line. It's even more dangerous in the pits on race day than it is during practice. . . . The speed in the pits should be a safe speed. I can't emphasize the fact enough that while it seems simple, an accident that takes place in the pits could be a very serious one indeed. And they're your friends there. You can multiply six or seven men times thirty-three, plus the other people that need to be in these pits, so make sure you have control of that car. . . . The fast lane is the outside lane, whether you're coming in or going out. And the slow lane is the inside lane. The pits are probably the most dangerous place on the racetrack."

The drivers shift in their seats.

Binford goes on: "You are aware that we have a red light. And it will be used in the event we have to put a red flag out and stop the race, in case of rain or some reason we have to stop the race. We hope it doesn't happen, but when that red light goes on, remember you're not being scored. You're not being scored. You can pull over to the side. You can pull into the pits at a slow pace. Take care of yourself. You're not racing when you see that red light."

Binford clenches and loosens his hands, then flits one up to his face. "Pushing and towing we've discussed at some length. You will be towed by a wrecker if you run out of fuel and you're mobile and you'll be taken all the way around, or you'll be met by a little tractor and that will bring you down to the head of the pits where your crews can get you there. We will not be able to do this, in all likelihood, after the hundred and ninetieth lap, because we have to use the yellow to protect you when we do this."

They know. They nod.

"I would ask that you be respectful to the emergency crews that are out there. They're out there for your benefit and they'll be under instructions by radio from us, so if they park you, we'll know about it. If they're wrong, we'll correct it. But don't get hot with them. They are trying to help you, and I'd appreciate your being respectful, as you normally are with them."

Binford pauses a moment.

"And now let's talk about the start. We've reviewed it. It's a simple procedure. When we start out on the first lap, the pace car will pull out after Tony Hulman's given the word. You will be lined up a hundred feet apart. It is important—emphasize important—that you maintain that interval. One of the most important safety moves that has been made here in the last two years—and we've had good starts in the last two years—has been the lengthening of that interval. So don't pack up. Keep that interval there. That's your safety valve. . . . You'll go at around 80 miles an hour maximum. You'll probably get up to 80 toward the third turn on the parade lap. And on the pace lap, we'll spot you at the same speed, about 80. The pace car will pull off as he comes through the fourth turn. He may get up to 90 miles an hour; hopefully you're cool enough that it won't be necessary to go any faster than that. At that point, you're under Johnny Rutherford's control, and he will bring you down, he tells me, at approximately the same speed. The green flag will be dropped if you are in line and as you come down finishing the pace lap. It will be dropped at a time probably after you pass somewhere between, oh, say the pit entrance and the starting line. If you are not lined up and we can't let you go, front line particularly, don't slow down but continue on through the first turn so that we don't pack up again, and re-form down the backstretch and Johnny will bring you around and we'll try it again. We're very hopeful that will not occur."

Binford pauses. He sweeps his gaze over the intent faces, sweat beading their brows. "Maintain those positions. And you all know that when you start the race there are lots of cars and lots of draft in there. There's very screwed-up air. It doesn't act the same as it does normally. So be cognizant of that fact when you come down into the first turn. I'm not telling you anything that you don't know, but there are a few rookies here, and I'm telling you what you've told me. . . . It's not going to be the same race car you've been driving in practice. You've got to get yourself sorted out. Except maybe for the first row, the real racing starts when you get over on the backstretch. Five hundred miles, two hundred laps, eight pit stops in all probability. There's no way you're going to win that race in the first turn, the second turn, or the first lap, or the second lap, and you can sure screw it up for yourselves and everybody else. The most important part if we're gonna have a good race tomorrow, we've got to have a good start."

Binford is sweating now, but he goes on. "If you do get in trouble, if you can't get in gear, your turbocharger won't kick in, hold your line. This will be true all through the race. If you're going slower than the car behind you and he's trying to pass you, hold your line. Don't try to move over for him, he might move into someone else. Hold your line and let them get around you."

Binford turns toward the homestretch. He gulps a breath and says, "I want to tell you that we think we have one of the finest fields of drivers and cars that we've ever had here. And I think that we're gonna have a great race. Gentlemen, you're gonna have a great race tomorrow. Have it. God bless all of you, and we'll see you afterward."

171

The meeting breaks up, the crowd dispersing in all directions, the drivers regrouping themselves out in front of the press room, where a bus is waiting to carry them downtown so they can take part in the annual parade.

★★★★★★★★★★★★★★★★

The parade moves through light drizzle. The drums and the horns and the cheers fill the air. People are happy. There is a spell of pure joy. Four hundred thousand people, or so runs the police estimate, rim the downtown streets of the city. Bob Hope, the grand marshal, wheels by in a car with track president Tony Hulman. A racket of applause. A float purrs by carrying the huge Borg-Warner Trophy, the busts of every race winner protruding from it, to be awarded to the winner tomorrow. Miniature replicas of Indianapolis cars, lined up in rows of three, their engines straining, chug by. The throb of the drums. Then an eagle cracking out of a shell on top of a float. Then the drivers, perched in the back seats of Buick convertibles, waving to the throngs. Some drivers are with their wives and children. A. J. Foyt is with a stuffed coyote between his knees.

The city of Indianapolis thrusts outward like a leaf, reaching across a level plain. Pressed in by low, sloping ridges, it straddles the White River and squats in the precise geographical center of the state. It is long on lovely sunsets and short on looks. Something like one million one hundred thousand people live here. Only nine other cities in the country claim more residents. It is pretty much devoid of things to do. Once it was the nation's car maker. Twenty-six makes in all, including the Duesenberg, the Marmon, the National, the Marion, the Stutz, the Pope. Indianapolis boomed as an automobile town. Sadly, Detroit was invented, and in the 1920s, bringing to bear its greater access to iron ore and cheap rail and water transportation, it knocked Indianapolis out of the car-production business. With no autos to sell, Indianapolis more or less fell asleep.

The city is somewhat of a grab bag, with the old and the new and the big plants and the glass buildings and the ranch types and the boardinghouses. Also, old department stores, dirty avenues, the grand hotels, the factories, wood houses with backyards, small motels, curvilinear private streets under yews and cedars, the remains of the stockyards, endless neighborhoods. Then, too, pawnshops, peep shows, and plastic quick-burger place after plastic quick-burger place. Downtown, poking two hundred and eighty-five feet into the sky, is the Soldier's and Sailor's Monument, raised there to memorialize the serviceman. A figure called Miss Indiana waves from the top.

The money in Indianapolis is made by manufacturing, by government, and by the wholesale and retail trade. People like to look on the place as the crossroads of the country. All roads shoot out from the monument; one heads directly east and west; you strike out on others and before you know it you stumble on Chicago or Detroit or Cincinnati or St. Louis, cities that encase Indianapolis in a giant box. It is fortunate for the roads. The city rose up on the White River largely because it was thought that water transportation was essential to the maturation of a great city. The river, as it turned out, is a dud. It's not navigable. Indianapolis is the biggest city in the country not placed on navigable water.

Inside the city, construction cranes crank and bulldozers with metal jaws take bites from the earth. There has been much construction in the last decade. Office buildings. Hotels. Apartments. Restaurants. Shopping centers. An immense sports arena—a thirty-million-dollar

174

complex, all shiny and new. The city sees itself as the next Houston or the next Atlanta, the next city to take off like a missile and become the talk of the nation. Its movers and shakers are prone to live in the future and to project their gray masses of numbers well forward. You hear more about 1990 than about next year.

The thing about the city is that people who don't live here tend to perceive it as a rotten place. The further away one gets, the worse it looks, hyperbole ballooning like bubble gum with distance. Pacing up and down in his office, William Hudnut, a gangling, moon-faced Presbyterian minister and the city's mayor, says, "I know. I know. I know what the image is. It's that we're one tremendous corn field. It's entirely correct. It's entirely correct for Indianapolis in the year 1920. It is not correct today. Look out that window. Do you see any corn fields?" In 1972, the Fantus Company, a research outfit which is good at profiling cities, put out an investor's report on Indianapolis, in the main because Indianapolis had asked for it and paid for the work. The report said both good and bad things. Among the former, it gave the city a "good to excellent" overall investor's rating. Among the latter was what it said about the city's image. This sort of thing: "Traditionally, Indianapolis has had the image of a somewhat straitlaced, unglamorous working town. While the city has changed greatly during the last decade, there is little evidence that its image has changed. In general, outsiders are unaware of the city's civic and cultural achievements and its impressive plans for future developments."

But then the city serves only as setting. To outsiders, everything that happens in Indianapolis seems to be closely bound up with the fortunes of the racetrack. The race took hold of Indianapolis and it won't let go. Many men, women, and children in the city are highly vocal, round-the-clock historians on the 500. Beyond the emotional impact, the Speedway has an economic effect on the area that is inestimable. Sales surge in everything.

175

Gasoline sells better. Clothing sells better. Advertising linage sells better. Pretzels sell better. Anacin sells better. Go down to the local Grand Union for a pound of butter, and you find Bobby Unser at the check-out counter. Come see the race, he says.

It is supposed that the city of Indianapolis hauls in eighteen million new dollars during the first twenty-eight days of the month and then a staggering eleven million dollars more over race weekend, when most people check into town. What helps yank in a considerable portion of this money is a spin-off of the race, the 500 Festival. Up till 1957, race fans would shuffle in weeks early for the big event, park their cars all around the Speedway, and start to party day and night. A carnival used to rise outside the grounds, offering rides, games, girlie shows, buttered popcorn. Civic leaders decided, why not give those early-arrivers something more organized and dignified to do, while at the same time funneling in some more tourist dollars for the city's coffers? A parade and a mayor's breakfast were put on in 1957, the sketchy outlines of a festival. Tony Hulman thought it was a silly idea that would never work. It has been going on ever since.

A full-time organization, 500 Festival Associates, operating out of spacious, downtown offices, today works year-round on the festival. Televised nationally on its own network, the parade now ranks second in size to the Tournament of Roses. The first event of the festival, though, gets under way in February, when three hundred thousands girls square off in the preliminary round of competition for the Festival Queen, a hotly contested crown in the state of Indiana. It is three months before the queen is actually crowned. Elsewhere in the city, events adhere to American tradition, featuring a radio-controlled car race at a shopping center on a miniature replica of the Indianapolis Motor Speedway, a gin rummy tournament, a bridge contest, a bubble-gum-blowing contest, a dress-up-like-mom parade, a look-like-your-favorite-television-personality event, an art show, a mayor's breakfast, a memorial service. For the parade, seven thousand square yards of black and white checkered Barwick Mills carpeting is spread over an entire block, curb-to-curb, on Pennsylvania Street, where national television cameras are set up. Thirty men work two hours taping the rug down. A big hunk of the carpet is sent over to where the Schlitz forty-horse hitch is stabled. For ten days, the horses practice prancing back and forth over the carpet. They had better. The first year the street was carpeted, the horses came up to it and stopped dead. They had to be dragged across.

Between twenty-five and thirty thousand people need hotel beds during the month. It is too many for total comfort. Altogether, the city's hotels and motels can handle nine thousand people. The Indianapolis Convention and Visitors Bureau puts people up in surrounding establishments, sometimes as distant as thirty miles from the track, and private homeowners offer rest for another two thousand racegoers. Lots of fans pull into town in mobile homes or elect to sleep under tents, and the track makes acres of parking space available for those so inclined. The Speedway itself operates the Speedway Motel, set alongside the track, but you better forget about getting rooms there. No one new has gotten space there in May since the opening of the motel fourteen years ago. The same race teams and accessory people who checked in that first year have renewed their reservations ever since. Any other month of the year, rooms go begging. Come in March and you don't need a reservation. Across the counter slides a room key. Fourteen dollars the night. Two months later, A. J. Foyt may sleep in your bed.

The 500 seems one of the givens in Indianapolis life, which is not to say that everyone likes it, or is in favor of it, or is proud of it. A certain subdued reservation about the race is apparent among a number of civic leaders and established citizens.

"The 500 gives the impression that the city is berserk about auto racing and very little else."

"An outsider is inclined to think that all we ever do is watch cars ripping around a track, that there is nothing to the city but roaring engines and smoking tires. That's ridiculous."

"We like cars. Sure we do. We also like theater. We also like museums. We also like movies. We also eat, sleep, work, and breathe."

"I know I'm the mayor of the city. But I'm also a minister. On race day, I'll be in church."

There is a feeling that the city needs to acquire an identity of its own. There are residents who have a considerable amount of time, energy, and money tied up in the place who in recent years have felt that the race is too big, that perhaps it is an obstacle to Indianapolis's gaining her deserved place among American cities. From the Fantus report: "Aside from the publicity generated by the 500, it is doubtful that this event contributes greatly to the image of Indianapolis as a community. The Speedway is the focus of national attention only once per year and for a very short period of time. Unlike a major cultural or educational institution, an automobile race does not strongly convey a positive impression of the quality of life in a community."

Ever since the report came out, civic leaders have gone to a good deal of fuss to explain why everyone should come to Indianapolis. The Chamber of Commerce began to pepper business publications with advertisements that pointed out some of the distinctive features of Indianapolis life. The boldest one read: "Indianapolis is lots of things besides the Indianapolis 500 race." Less bold variations would go: "Indianapolis is the home of the biggest children's museum in the world" or "Indianapolis is the biggest 4-H center in the country." A Chamber of Commerce moving force said one afternoon, "We don't even like the word Indy, because that connotes the track. We don't look at ourselves as a community built around a race. It's just not that way. People have warped this whole thing. We don't want to be mean to the 500. It's all

178

right. I sometimes go to it, and boy, those cars really do move. But people live here three hundred and sixty-four other days of the year. The city doesn't have a million people shoot out of the ground one day a year. The city would not up and die if they stopped that race."

★★★★★★★★★★★★★★★★

Less than twenty-two hours till the race, and the engine of car number 93, roosting on the wheeled table, is being warmed up inside the garage. It throbs raucously and sprays noise off the walls of the garage, killing talk. After arriving late last night, the engine was bolted into place at six this morning, perhaps the last engine in the starting field to go into its car. Flopped on his back, Bill Finley is crawling around underneath number 93, completing its final prerace checkout. He has been there most of the day. His eyes move from weld to weld. Finally, he emerges from under the car and says he thinks everything is ready. He cuts the engine. The radio is spewing music into the cool, oily dampness.

Vatis says, "What do you figure for mileage?"

Finley says, "Probably 1.8."

"Mm," Vatis says.

"We could start out settling for 1.7 to get more speed, then see about caution flags and go from there," Barnes says.

Finley says, "Yeah, yeah, that would be good."

Johnny Parsons, back from the parade, sallies in.

"Why don't you pop in, kid, and try it out," Finley says.

Parsons frugs into the cockpit and samples the clutch, the throttle, the brake pedal. "Seems fine. Seems fine," he says. He clamps the seat belt and the shoulder harness around him to make sure they are all right. "If you don't like anything," Finley says, "you know you can just hand me your hat." A raft of people is billowing by in the walkways of Gasoline Alley, peering into the stalls, as if trying to sniff out a winner. Some men carry children astride their necks to see over the crowd.

Steve Krisiloff comes in with his arm twined around a pretty woman with a dairymaid complexion.

"What, a different girl?" Finley says with a lopsided grin.

"Nope, same one."

"That's a different girl," Finley persists, brow gone all quirky.

"Oh, you're getting old."

Vatis says, "Where I come from we're allowed five."

Finley says, "What are you, Arabs?"

"Yeah, first cousins."

Shorty is cutting numbers out of magnetized paper to be used on the pit board. After he gets done with a letter, he heaves it back over his shoulder toward the metal closet in the corner, where it hits and sticks with a thunk. Numbers fastened at every conceivable angle to it, the cabinet has the look of a tote board gone wild. Finley scoops up a sugar doughnut and starts chomping on it. He hoists a cup of coffee. Barnes slobbers away an apple and then licks the tips of his fingers.

"The countdown's beginning," Barnes says. "You can feel the tension already. On race day, when the cars are lined up out on the track, when everywhere you look there are people, there are energy forces you feel out there beside your car that you can't believe. There's never been a year when I haven't cried."

Some people from Ayr-Way pad into the garage. They hand over a blown-up photograph of all the crew members, signed by Ayr-Way officials, wishing the team good luck. They shake hands all around.

"Bring her on home, boys."

"We want to see that trophy right over there."

"It'll be there."

Lounging on an overturned box, Parsons is mulling his strategy for the start, building for himself a psychology of victory. From his spot in the middle of the fifth row, it is easy to get boxed in by other cars. The key car is the one starting directly in front of you, in Parsons' case that of Mike Mosley. Parsons plans to blast straight ahead, following Mosley, if he manages a good start. Sometimes Mosley has trouble getting through his gears and is not an aggressive starter. Parsons knows this from having started behind him in the past. Parsons is aggressive, something he has picked up from running sprint cars and midgets, where it's important to gain spots right off because the races are short. If Mosley has trouble, then Parsons plans to go to the right, where there are more assertive starters. He expects to have the men on each side of him beat, and if he gets a half car length advantage on them, they'll have to "give him the racetrack." By the time he is through the first turn, Parsons hopes to have gained maybe three or four spots, and to come around after the first lap in eleventh or tenth. With good pit stops—fourteen to eighteen seconds—and with a healthy engine, he expects to be in the top five by a quarter of the race and to have "pretty good" odds of winning. In his mind, fifteen men could win, with Foyt, Al Unser, Rutherford, and Andretti the main men to beat.

Vatis is asked about his feelings on the race.

"I feel rather optimistic," he says. "You never know in racing. I think we'll be top five. With a couple of breaks, we have an outside shot. It could happen. It could happen tomorrow. We've got the best chance we've ever had."

"How about the engine?"

Vatis smiles warily. "I'm not really sure it will last. You take risks in this business."

The conversation drifts to things that might go wrong during five hundred miles.

"Anything can happen, hundreds of things. This is a

breakdown race. It's long and punishing and it takes a lot of cars."

"You can do the most meticulous preparation there is, spend all the money and go out on the first lap. It's an impossible race to win."

"Look at Mario Andretti. He's come here with the best cars, the best mechanics, tons of money. Four out of the last five years, he's gone out before fifty laps were run. Three of the times not a dozen laps were gone."

"In 1967, Parnelli Jones had the race in his pocket when with four laps to go a fifty-cent bolt broke on his car and Foyt won."

"It's been figured that running this race at these kinds of speeds is like fifty thousand miles of highway driving. You can see why things break."

"Sometimes not even ten cars go the distance."

"Anything can happen in the last hours before the race. Two years ago, someone swiped Foyt's driving suit from his garage. There were only a couple of hours before the start. It almost looked like he'd have to pull out. Luckily, someone dug up an old suit that barely fit him."

A gulf of quiet follows. Barnes digs his hands into his pockets. Finley rocks from foot to foot and wrings an oil rag in his hand. Vatis sighs, makes a few aimless sputters with his lips. Scooping up his jacket, he takes his leave.

"Well, see you in the morning, boys."

"Take it easy, boss," Barnes calls. "Don't worry too much."

"The day I stop worrying will be the day I stop racing."

The afternoon drones on. Piece by piece, the car is slapped back together. Tires go on. The cowl goes on. Five rear body sections go on. The engine cover. The nose. At 2:45 Finley leaves for home.

"If you need me, I'll be home fidgeting," he says. He looks bushed; his eyes are bleary.

"Okay," Barnes says.

Krisiloff gets ready to go. He takes a wadded handkerchief from his pocket and knocks it against his nose.

"Don't stay out too late," Parsons says.

"I won't."

"Don't be too tired."

"You neither," Krisiloff says, grinning.

"I'm never too tired."

Krisiloff gazes down at Parsons' car.

"Is she ready?"

"We'll find out tomorrow," Parsons says, emptying out his ear.

"Looks ready."

"I'll know by the first corner," Parsons says.

Krisiloff trudges off, and a short while later, Parsons leaves.

"See you tomorrow, John," Barnes says.

"Yeah, I'll see. Depends if I'm not too busy."

Barnes and Butch Meyer continue to putter with the car. Most of the other garages are silent and locked as night approaches, offering small indication of what will take place tomorrow. The Gasoline Alley crowd dissolves. Some crew members are bedding down inside their garages, better to do that than fight the throngs tomorrow morning. There is a grace and dispensation in the air, excitement and hope about the race tomorrow.

"You worried, John?" someone asks.

Barnes shrugs and waves a cloud of bugs away. "No point in being worried. You worry now and you're dead. We've done all we can do. I feel we've done a good job. We've prepared as well as you can. You know, you work and work, and then when the race comes, you got to just concentrate on your job that day. If you're not in total concentration on race day you're dead. My job is changing that right-rear tire, and that's all I'll be thinking about. You don't worry about what can go wrong. It's too late. Nothing you can do. Race day, it's up to God."

★★★★★★★★★★★★★★★★

The sides of the camper are royal blue, bearing the sign, INDY OR BUST. A small, monkey-faced man is up front. He has a wart on the side of his nose. Another man alongside him is playing a wheezing harmonica. "We gonna drink tonight," the monkey-faced man says. "Lord, oh Lord, we gonna drink some whiskey tonight."

His friend, a prissy-voiced grasshopper of a man, hesitates in his playing and croaks, "This is a privilege to be here. Yes, it is my great privilege to be here." A moth bumps against the harmonica. He brushes it aside and starts playing again.

The night is not nearly over, and the sidewalks are mobbed with people puffing by, feet slapping on the pavement. The crowd passes with a tidal motion, eddying very slowly to who knows where; it just moves. The streets are convulsed with traffic, cars frog-marching down the asphalt, moving under the yellowy blobs of light thrown downward by street lamps, neon winking. Miles down the roads bordering the track, in the grassy areas, everywhere you look, cars and campers are parked. Tents are up. Bonfires streak the darkness. There are stars in the sky, and the air is thick as syrup. A siren hoots once. At five o'clock tomorrow morning, a bomb will explode, and the gates to the track will swing open, and the cars and the people will storm in. But that is hours from now; there is time to be whittled away.

There is the air of carnival. Stands hawking all manner of souvenirs, drinks, and food have gone up along the roadways. The freaked-out are here in great numbers, perambulating down this rag-tag midway; the men and women all dressed alike: work shirts and jeans, many without shoes. Action is on in the night. Amid the flood of people moving in front of the Speedway is a young man in a white shirt and dark pants thumbing out slips of pink paper. On one side is a picture of Wilbur Shaw, three-time winner of the race, slouched behind the wheel of a Maserati. On the reverse is a tract, entitled "Who Will Win the Race?" and concerned with the Race of Life.

Dozens of people, young and old, are slumped in tubular beach chairs, hard against Sixteenth Street, gawking at the people in the cars rumbling past. The license plates are from all over; in the space of a few minutes, one can see cars from Michigan, California, Arizona, New York, Pennsylvania, New Jersey, Texas, Nebraska. There are some dilapidated old cars and trucks and many new Cadillacs, Chryslers, and Buicks. A caravan of four New Jersey cars worms by. The people in the cars gape at the people in the chairs. They holler back and forth at each other.

"Hey, want a lift? Come on, hop right in the back."

"Where you from? Where is you from?"

"I ain't from anywhere."

"That's where I'm from."

"Hey, who are you?"

"Beats me. Who am I?"

Four young men and women, dressed in jeans and barefoot, are clustered in a circle and they are screaming into the night air: "Heeeeeeee-hooooooooooo." They crane for the echo. Then they sound off again at the top of their voices, an ear-splitting scream: "Heeeeeeeee-Hooooooooooo." Nearby, while chicken soup warms on a Coleman stove, a group is puttering at badminton, over a net strung between two campers. "C'mon, hit that birdie, Lawrence. Lawrence, hit the damn thing!"

A man is sitting in his car, gabbing on the phone. The man is middle-aged, maybe forty. There are pale half-moons dipping below his shades. He explains that he is calling his wife in Texas. She didn't care to make the trip. Says she'll catch the race on television. Who will win tomorrow?

"I'm looking for Rutherford. Rutherford seems the one. He's got the car. He's got the desire. I think the man will take it. You can't figure this race, though. It's a car beater. Rutherford might blow on lap one. Sure would make me unhappy. Mostly come to see him." He yawns a little and pulls at his nose. Then he goes back to yakking with his wife. "And you know what happened then . . ."

There is more and more turbulence on the streets. People are piling up empty beer cans—mostly Budweiser and Schlitz—into a beer-can pyramid along Sixteenth Street. Twenty, thirty, fifty cans go up. "Let's go for the moon," a man yells. "No, make it Mars." Sixty, seventy cans pile up. Then the pyramid collapses, Budweiser and Schlitz cans clanking onto the street, rolling under cars.

There is a brisk trade in souvenirs. Sexy T-shirts. Wild T-shirts. Jeans for three bucks. Cutoffs for two. A confection of jewelry items, marked down 30 percent. Flags, hats, toy race cars. Pillows. Banners. Belts. Buckles. Toy Goodyear blimps. More T-shirts—Slave Master, Do-It-in-a-Van, Born to Lose, Duster, Pinball. Mr. Weirdo novelties. Chicken puppets. And refreshments are selling. Wendy's Chili and Frosting. Hot dogs on a stick. Corn dogs. Lemonade. Corn on the cob. Foot-long hot dogs. Popcorn. Mister Softie.

An educational Marine Life Display is housed in a trailer. A prim-voiced barker, a man in a khaki shirt, stands outside urging people to augment their knowledge of the world by going in and looking at a man-eating shark. "Go in and take a peek," his voice burbles cheerfully. "Sneak a look at the shark. Ya won't believe it. It's a memorable sight. See that shark."

Volunteers for disabled veterans are passing out literature and flag pins. "Will you wear the flag for a disabled veteran?" Across from the Speedway's main gate, the White Castle fast-food stand is doing voluminous business. Lines at every counter. "I can't get your burger any faster," says a pasty-faced waitress. "I'm not the stove." Pariah dogs snarl over leavings in the back of the stand. Close by, old Rosner's Drugstore, a stark brick structure, is brimming with patrons. Amid the bobby pins and the toothpaste and the Ban underarm, people reach out for their sodas. "Over here's the chocolate malted. Deliver me that chocolate malted."

Down Georgetown Road, a scalper is on the prowl. "Who needs a ticket?" he shouts. "Get your tickets here."

"How much?"

"Twenty bucks."

"What do they go for?"

"Five."

Farther on, three men who appear to be in their twenties are clucking alongside their van, drinking can after can of beer. Sixteen cases, a hundred and ninety-two cans of beer, are stacked up in the back of the van. Behind the men weaves the White River. The water looks like Monel Metal. A cluster of sitting waterfowl blackdots the slick gray surface.

"This here is the only race we come to, and the only one we ever will," one of the group says. "It's our ninth year. I don't know why we come. It's hard to explain feelings about this place. I guess the party end of it has a lot to do with it, all the interesting people and all. We always have a blast. And, of course, this here is the biggest sporting event in the world."

"Last year, I fell into a little bit of trouble," one of the others says. "You see, this guy walloped me. I smacked him. Two cops grabbed me. I kicked the cops. The cops didn't like that. They put me in a straitjacket. No fun at all."

"These cars, you know, just have this magnetic appeal," the third man says. "I don't go for the other kinds of racing. But you see these monsters, hear their engines purr, and it's something else. This race, it just thrills the life out of me. I never feel better than when I see that start. I intend to see it as long as I've got eyes."

"We've seen some super wrecks here, too," the first man says. "Saw the one where Swede Savage wiped out his car. Saw the one with Salt Walther—almost burned himself to death. Last year, we was right near where Tom Sneva took that awful flip. Thought the man was dead. Now, here he is, on the front row for tomorrow. Racing is something. I'll tell you, these guys got guts. Got to have guts to step into one of those brutes."

A purveyor of fluorescent necklaces pads by. His breath stinks from bourbon and cigars. He was introduced to the business by his father-in-law. Been in it now for seven years. "You can make a fortune in neon necklaces," he says. "It is a growth industry."

At the Classic Motor Lodge, the lounge is jumping with a live rock band, every table is full, and the dance floor is clogged with swirling bodies. Bobby McGee is belting out the songs. "Come on, rock your baby. Yeah, yeah, rock your baby." Husky waitresses weave through the tightly packed tables, their trays brimming with highballs, beers. The walls and carpet are green. Green is bad luck in auto racing. No race drivers, mechanics, or car owners are here. They are all in bed. Many of the people who are here will for sure have trouble recognizing a race car in the morning.

Who will win tomorrow?

"Andretti's my man," says a chap hunkered at a back table, working on his fifth vodka, the empty glasses forming a fortress before him. He has a full, youthful, clever face. His pop eyes are riveted on an eye-stingingly beautiful brunette. "Mario's got his act together this time.

It don't matter he's stuck in the back of the pack. When you can run, you could be dead last at the green and you can take her. The 500 is a grind, though. So many things can happen. All those guys want to win so bad. They'd run over their grandmothers to win this one."

The hours ache on. People are sitting on roofs of cars, bumpers, hoods. A man and a porcine girl are sprawled under a blanket on the hood of a black Buick, sound asleep, snores billowing out of their mouths as thousands chuff by. A man is leaning against a rusted van, a parrot in a cage next to him. "Parrot wants Foyt. I want Rutherford."

At the fringe of the field where Sixteenth Street transects Georgetown Road, on a flatbed truck, a wide-eyed man in his sixties is trying to spread the good word of the Lord. A plantation of fine graying hair hangs to shoulder length from the man's bald crown, giving him the look of a mad chemist.

"Now you men and women, you have got to show your faith, you have got to please God tonight. Not tomorrow, but tonight. If you don't start this night, when then? You there, boy. Would you like to be called a child of God? Come be called a child of God. Nothin' to be scared of. Step on up. And you, young fella? Will you overcome the world? God is good, ladies and gentlemen, and we must show Him our faith. How 'bout you, young lady? Will you see the light?"

A tall stringy man nearby, a lickerish look on his face, holds up two empty hands and shows both sides to onlookers in an impromptu magic show. Suddenly, he has a red ball the size of a bing cherry in his hand. A second one sprouts into view. Nothing is up his sleeve. He has no sleeve. He is bare-chested.

Three small kids squat on the top of a Winnebago, Tennessee plates, hollering down at people passing in dizzying spirals: "Who do you want to win? Who do you want to win?"

The answers come back in many pitches of voice.

190

"Al Unser."

"Foyt."

"Andretti."

"Scratch me for Foyt."

"A. J."

"Sneva."

"Ole Bobby Unser."

"Rutherford. Yessir, Johnny Rutherford."

Sympathies shoot all across the starting lineup.

The night is sticky, nearly midnight now, the night moving onward into the witching hours. Only a few lights show from the windows of the motels. Under the street lights, the ragged figures all have a somber uniformity, the cars grinding and backfiring beside them. The noises keep ringing through the air.

★★★★★★★★★★★★★★★★

Butch Meyer is first to arrive in garage number 65. He slopes in at four-thirty. He couldn't get home last night. He lives only a few blocks from the track in the Georgetown Apartments, but police turned him back because of rioting. A car was ignited. A hundred people were arrested. So he went over and bedded down at his father's and has arrived with him. Bill Finley and Reny saunter in at five. Finley got to bed at seven and intended to wake up at three, but he overslept and didn't awaken till four-fifteen, when Reny came by from next door and jerked him out of slumber.

"How ya sleep, Bill?" Butch asks.

"I didn't sleep much last night," Finley says weakly. "Last night was worry night."

Dew is heavy on the grass beside the long rows of garages. The early sunlight glistens on the roofs and crewmen range along the outer edge of the fence. It is a ghostly hour. Spectator cars are piling into the infield now, darting and weaving into preferred viewing spots. Traffic worms slowly outside the gates. Sidewalks are muddled with people, all padding in the same direction, toward the Indianapolis Motor Speedway. Every square inch of concrete and asphalt is glutted with cars and buses and people moving at a turgid pace. Kids shouldering coolers and blankets, girls in tight cut-offs. The mob is thick for many blocks around the track. Cars are parking in people's front lawns, five dollars apiece. Haggard old women and jut-jawed men are on the street wagging big signs: PARK HERE, calling out in reedy voices. "Lot of room, right near the hedges, ya get out in no time."

Few sounds break the stillness of the stalls—stamping of feet, muffled coughs. Every so often, the clacking of wrenches in garages chops into the silence. TV and radio men are shuffling by. TV coverage will be broadcast tonight to most of the United States, with an audience of thirty-two million expected. Live radio coverage, from Sid Collins, a local sportscaster known as "The Voice of the 500," is expected to reach two hundred million people. Some of the doors along the rows of stalls are still shut and locked. A number are empty; quite a few of the unqualified machines have already been shipped home. Thirty-three house race cars ready to run. One of them will win today. All the dreams will come true. A chance of rain is forecast in the afternoon. The air is chill.

One by one, the rest of the crew troops in: Shorty, Texas, Hoyt. Last night, Mike Herion curled up in his car in the garage-area parking lot to escape the twenty-minute commute home. Shorty eventually goes and jogs him into awareness. John Barnes comes in. The gate designated for race crews is badly congested, and Barnes got hopelessly snarled in the bog of cars.

"Hey, kid," Finley says cheerfully. "Heard you were stuck in line."

Barnes says, "Whole teams are out there. I never saw anything so messed up. I finally just whipped down the sidewalk and put the car on a guy's lawn for five bucks. Then I walked in."

Finley wrinkles his forehead. "This is gonna piss you off when I tell you what I did. I overslept."

Barnes blurts out a laugh.

"You know what happened to me?" Finley says. He speaks around a toothpick without really looking up.

"The guard wouldn't let me in the gate. 'Uh-uh, I'm going in there,' I told him. 'What for?' he says. 'Well, see, they've got a race here today—you heard about it—and I'm the crew chief on one of the cars.' So he still says, 'Can't do it.' 'Well, I'm gonna spin out,' I says. And I backed up and turned around and came in. The crew from Rutherford's car was there walking in, they had abandoned their truck, so I told them to hop in the back and we all drove in."

"If Rutherford wins, it's your fault," Barnes says.

Finley checks the holes in the wheels to make sure the pins will fit in place when the tires are changed. He moves slowly, dragging each wheel from a stack of tires. Very gently, he pokes his fingers into the holes. Butch is warming up the oil in number 92; it has to be heated for about a half hour, till it reaches a temperature of close to two hundred degrees, the running temperature. Barnes begins to pile up tires on a long wheeled rack that will be rolled out to the pits to hold the spare tires during the race.

Matt Murphy clomps in.

"Morning, gentlemen."

"Is it?" Finley says.

Hoyt begins to load up a three-level cart, like a hostess serving cart, with two air wrenches, two vent bottles, four pit boards, a spare wrench. He wheels it out to the pit apron.

Barnes jacks up the front of number 93 and screws on two front chassis pieces and the nose. Butch warms up the engine on number 92. He starts and stops it in a jerky fashion. Chug-a-chug. Chug-a-chug. Chug-a-chug. Then a steady roar. Vroooooom! This lets the oil flow through the engine and lubricate it. Reny pulls a cart with the starter on it out to the pits. Meanwhile, Texas tugs two Igloo five-gallon coolers from their cardboard boxes, then fills them with cold water for the crew during the race. The crew continues to order things, eroding the clifflike minutes with waves of noncommittal activity. Few words are needed for the action.

Finley looks at the Valvoline clock: five minutes to six o'clock.

Near the back fence of Gasoline Alley, a minister is delivering a sermon from the rear of a battered red pickup. Clad in a white robe, he is talking into a microphone propped up on a small wooden table. Two candles glimmer from the table and two young boys are standing stiffly, one to each side. Around thirty men mill in front of the truck.

"For all those who will be gathering for the sixtieth running of the Indianapolis 500-mile race, that it may be for them a safe and enjoyable day, we praise the Lord. For all the drivers, mechanics, and all others associated with the running of this great race, that it may be safe we praise the Lord. For all those who have died and gone to their eternal rest, especially those who have died in the sport of automobile racing and those who have given their lives in the service of their country that we memorialize this week, we praise the Lord. . . ."

Barnes starts heating the oil in 93. He checks the spark plugs. Engines begin to thrum in other garages; people stream by. Finley hoists a cup of coffee and puts it away. He pulls a cigarette away from his package of Salems, lights it, and takes a drag. Shorty flicks on the radio; Linda Ronstadt pounds out. Everyone is trying to keep busy, to reduce the tension. The tension hangs in the air like rain clouds.

It's 6:45 on the Valvoline clock. The crew wheels the 92 to the fueling station to fill up the tank.

"Fill up this thing with about sixty gallons," Butch says.

"Yeah, you and thirty-two others."

Matt and Reny begin to polish the 93 with rags and Blue Max Cleaner Wax. They slop the soggy rags over the frame, like attendants at a dollar car wash. Shorty piles the Shopper's Fair wagon with assorted rags and spare gloves and tools that might be needed and leaves for the pit apron, yawning.

"Wake up, Shorty."

"I'll wake up in Victory Lane."

Doubled over, Barnes is carefully smoothing white tape over the joints in the body parts and over the screws that bolt the pieces to the chassis.

"What's that do, John?" someone asks.

"It keeps the body from vibrating a bit," he says. He hesitates a moment. "And, mainly, it keeps you from getting nervous as hell. Want some?"

Last night, Barnes went home and "did the usual May 30 deal. I got the nervous shits."

Now Matt polishes the two rearview mirrors. Finley tightens the lug nuts on the wheel. Car 92 returns full of fuel, and Shorty and Butch start applying Blue Max to it. "Three hundred thousand people gonna look at that car today," Shorty says. "You want it to be pretty." Barnes starts chugging the engine on number 93.

Standing nearby, Hoyt spits out a toothpick and says, "The first ten laps is hell. All I ever remember is the first ten laps and the first pit stop. After that, I don't remember anything. You're so busy. Last year, I never heard them play the National Anthem."

A call comes from the loudspeakers: "Your attention in the garage area. All cars must be on the pit apron by eight o'clock. Attention in the pit area. All cars must be on the pit apron by eight o'clock."

Finley's ears prick up. "Gosh, I thought it was eight-thirty."

At 7:45 Tassi Vatis clumps in, slightly sleep-rumpled, wearing dark pants, a blue striped shirt and a blue racing jacket. He sits down, slitting his eyes and stroking his head.

"Hello, Tassi. Did you have any trouble getting up this morning?"

"I was up last night."

Following dinner at his hotel, Vatis turned in early but couldn't sleep much. "You never sleep well before this race. You're not so much worrying as hoping. You're hoping things go your way. You're hoping maybe this time you hit it." After hours of tossing, Vatis awoke around five, got his family together, munched some breakfast, and walked over to the track.

"You'll look good, in Victory Lane with the cameras popping at you."

"If I'm in Victory Lane, I won't see any cameras."

It is 8:08. The crew rolls number 93 to the fueling pumps, where a long line of cars waits for servicing. Others, fueled up, pass by on their way to the pits. Barnes settles down on the side of the car and fingers the corner of his moustache. Finley remains standing, puffing a Salem. He works his hands down into his pockets.

"Well," Finley says softly. "The pot's on the goose."

Barnes nods.

"No more yesterdays, todays, or tomorrows. Only this afternoon."

The car reaches the fuel island, and a hose clanks into the tank.

Barnes says to Finley, "What did we figure on pit stops?"

"Bring this in at twenty-five laps, the other car at twenty-seven, and not deviate from that more than five laps all day."

"Good."

"If there's a yellow at twenty, fine. If seventeen, nope. Stay out there."

"Yeah, we've had a lot of luck with that system."

Again there is the voice quaking on the loudspeakers, urging the crews to bring their cars to the pit apron.

The fuel tank full, Finley and Barnes start wheeling number 93 out to the pits. Number 92 has already been pushed out. As they move past other crewmen, they wish each other luck.

"Good luck, Bill."

"Luck Jim."

"Have some luck, John."

"You too, Larry."

Bands are surefootedly making their way down the straightaway, marching to the strains of trumpets and drums, as Parsons' crew rolls the car down the concrete apron. Flutes warbling, drums sounding, sweet music, dancing girls, and the racers being pushed into line. The stands are slowly filling with people, some sections are already packed. A phalanx of mass-media representatives are swooping about. There are friends and wives and relatives about—a muted festivity is in the air.

Parsons' pit is about two-thirds of the way down toward the fourth turn. Finley and Barnes confirm the air pressure in the tires, then slap the impounded rubber from qualifying day back on the car, putting the other tires neatly in place on the tire rack. Part of the crew lumbers out to the pit wall to view the bands and majorettes as they prance by. The bands seem to have no end. Vatis and his wife sit silently on the wall between the two cars. The Purdue University band presses by, trailed by a Ford pickup with the world's largest drum in the back. Every now and then, a man wallops it. Two hours, a little less, till the race.

Finley says, "This is like seeing your sweetheart off for the last time. You've taken her to the airport. Her plane is ready to take off. You stand there. You'll never run this Indianapolis 500 again."

At 9:40 Johnny Parsons straggles out to his pit, clad in a pair of jeans and a sport shirt. Last night, he went to a midget race at a local speedway, left before the main event, and turned in by eleven. His wife was still doing her hair. Two years ago, Parsons' first race here, he couldn't sleep at all the night before. He paced. He tossed in his sleep. On the way over to the track with his wife and parents, he couldn't sit still. He started coughing, complaining that the air was causing him to gag. They plodded into traffic. Unable to take it any longer, Parsons got out and walked in.

Parsons huddles with the crew to chat about pit strategy.

Finley: "When I get finished changing your right tire, if I ever get finished, and if Barnes does your right rear, because he was pretty drunk last night, then I'll be collapsing just past the front of your car. From the ground, I'll wave to you to go out."

Parsons: "You won't be blocking my way?"

Finley: "Nah, I'll just be out of the way."

Barnes: "You can nudge him a little if you want."

Finley: "So I'll signal, and you'll be out of here in about two minutes."

Parsons: "Great!"

At a quarter to ten, the pit crews begin to wheel the race cars out to their starting positions on the track proper. The stands are crammed by now. The sound of the crowd keeps rising as race time grows closer, people speculating to one another on what is to come. That Foyt is bound to be getting impatient. Wins the race three out of seven years and now has gone eight years without another one. He's just going to blast out front and take off like a scalded dog. Rutherford can't be touched. He is loaded for bear. He can't forget the rain last year; he knows that race was his. Andretti will be in the lead inside of ten laps. He's sick of dropping out. He'll fly through the pack like water through a sieve. Sneva could surprise a lot of folks. Every day out here, he's been getting a little faster. He's got the car to win. Be nice to see a former school principal take the biggest auto race in the world. The best car out there is Al Unser's. For quality of equipment that is the best car. Al's got to want that third win. His owner is Parnelli Jones, who won the race in 1963 and should have won it a couple of other times. It's a team to beat. Johncock wants it awfully bad. The year he won it was the second shortest race in history, rained out after a hundred and thirty-three laps. He wants to win a full one. To boot, he just got married and what a wedding gift this would make. Johncock's got the best mechanic in the world, George Bignotti. Bignotti's cars have won this race six times. Nobody else has a record that can touch that. With a teammate like Wally Dallenbach, who led this race much of the way last year, the Bignotti-tuned cars are going to be tough as nails. What about Parsons? He's a long shot all right, but maybe. The Greek is one man who's been hurting to win this race a long time. Odder things have happened. How did Opperman get in this race and in that car? You can't figure it. The race takes all kinds.

They are all on the track now—a hundred and thirty-two wheels, thirty-three cars, two hundred crewmen. Still in his street clothes, Parsons tries on his helmet. He has a loop of cord bolted to the left side, through which he now threads his left shoulder; it will hold his head from being thrown to the right through the corners. A man's neck can wear out after five hundred miles of left turns.

The engines are warmed up out on the track for five minutes. The air throbs with the noise. Then they are shut off, coughing and expiring in patches. At 10:20 Parsons heads back to the garage to peel off his clothes and pull on his uniform, waiting till the last moment to avoid the tension-building festivities. The first year, he was covered with goose pimples and thought he might faint on the track.

Parsons and Krisiloff come back together, and the crew wishes Krisiloff luck as he moves back to his starting position. "Have a good race, Steve." Parsons is sipping slowly from a can of Gatorade, Pam next to him prettily dressed in a white pants suit.

"What time is it?" Parsons says.

"Ten-thirty."

"What time they putting us in the cars?"

200

"About ten minutes."

Jerry Grant, who is starting from the ninth row, jounces by. "It'll take me three laps to catch you," he says to Parsons.

"That long?"

Parsons presses a pair of spare glasses on Texas. "Leave them in the garage. I'll get them after I pick up the trophy and everything."

Duane Carter, Parsons' stepfather, comes by, peers at Parsons, points his finger at the side of his head, then walks off. Pam comes up and kisses and hugs Parsons; then she drifts back to the stands to watch the race with some friends.

Bands break into the National Anthem, then a lone bugler plays taps in memory of our war dead and the men whose lives the track has taken. Finally, "Back Home Again in Indiana." Crewmen pat the drivers on the back; they nod. Bombs explode, shaking the air, and ten thousand colored balloons soar into the clouds over the track. The sound from the crowd swells, becoming a scream. Settling his helmet on his head, Parsons looks over his shoulder at the balloons rising and climbs into the car. The crew buckles him in. To himself, he says a prayer for a safe race and for his own good fortune.

In a quaky voice, Tony Hulman gives out the historic words: "Gentlemen . . . start . . . your engines." The din from the grandstands is deafening. The engines churn to life, the roar impossible to describe—a rasp, thunder, and rumble like that of a hundred freight trains passing at once. The crewmen on Parsons' car lift their right arm in the air to signal to the pace car that the engine has started. All the engines are running. Parsons looks to his left. His father raises a thumb and moves back over the wall.

Slowly, the pace car eases away. The cars are pushed off, falling into their rows of three. The crew members, lugging the starter engines, rush back to the pits, like a mob scene in a movie, as the cars pound through the first turn on the first of two buildup runs. The field swishes around now on the parade lap, the cars sheering from side to side, a way to heat up the tires to give them better adhesion. As the field files past the big grandstands, the drivers wave to the audience. The crowd, on its feet, wags handkerchiefs and caps and programs at the men in the cars, all the while cheering madly. Next time around, the race will start.

★★★★★★★★★★★★★★★★

The green flag. A tremendous bellow and a dizzying flash of color, and the field plunges down the straightaway toward the first corner, like a hive of bees in chase of honey. The start is a frightening spectacle that no other sport approaches. Thirty-three automobiles, fifteen hundred pounds each, eight hundred horsepower, practically welded together, side by side and tail to nose on a cramped ribbon of asphalt at close to 200 miles per hour, hitting the first curve hard. Such air suction develops that cars in the thick of the pack would be jerked through the first corner even if the driver failed to touch the throttle. Champions do not try bold things here. Not on the start. They wait. It is the most difficult and dangerous moment. Difficult to maneuver a car in and dangerous for oneself. Many spectators will not look at the cars till they know they are safely through the first turn. But this is a superlative start. The cars in tight, orderly formation. Johnny Rutherford and Gordon Johncock charge side by side for the corner. Tom Sneva, on the outside of the front row, lags back a couple of car lengths. A. J. Foyt muscles ahead of Al Unser and Pancho Carter in row two. Johnny Parsons, following Mike Mosley straight ahead, whips past Bobby Unser and then draws outside of Larry "Boom Boom" Cannon and sprints past him. In this order, the cars pile into the first turn: Rutherford ahead, Johncock close behind, Sneva third, Foyt fourth. The noise is enough to jar the world. They run nose to tail through the corner, then sweep out high and into the short chute.

"And they're safely through turn number one. Safely through turn number one," crackle the loudspeakers. A screech goes up from the crowd. Whistling, clapping, cheers. In 1966, there was a fourteen car pileup, tires and wreckage strewn all across the homestretch, before the field had gotten this far. As the pack pounds through the short straightaway between the first and second corners, still tightly bunched, through turn two and into the backstretch, Rutherford stretches his advantage to three car lengths.

On the front straightaway, without even crossing the starting line to receive the green flag, Spike Gehlhausen, at twenty-one the youngest man in the race, has become its first casualty. Gehlhausen swoops immediately into the pits. His mechanics take a look at the engine. He wiggles out of the car, undoes his helmet, and clumps behind the pit wall, grimly disappointed. The engine went. A month of racing, a year of planning for this. He didn't even get to make the first turn. For him, the race lasted ten seconds. It can be that cruel.

Coming around to complete lap one of the race, Rutherford has patched together a five-car-length lead over Johncock; his yellow car leads Johncock's day-glo red; number 2 leads number 20. The race is a minute old, and Rutherford is five car lengths in the lead. The field is stringing out behind him. There is a wave of cheering from the crowd. Sneva stands a car length behind Johncock, then Foyt breathing down his tailpipe, then Carter smack behind him. Having passed two more cars already, Parsons is tenth. As the pack makes for the first turn, Foyt ducks under Sneva and jockeys into third. Down the backstretch, Foyt pulls up alongside Johncock, his engine really stitching, and bursts ahead. He is clawing for the lead. The crowd bubbles with glee. A big portion of the audience would like to see Foyt write history today. At this point, he seems to have the quickest machine on the track. Lengths behind another car at the beginning of the front straightaway, he will gobble up ground with ease and be hard on the car's exhaust pipe by the turn. Then he will slide around and begin to pull away. Foyt's strength is his straightaway power. Still, there are four hundred and ninety-six miles to go.

Overlooking the racers on the starting platform, Pat Vidan is a study in concentration, trolling with his eyes for signs of trouble. He can see only a scant portion of the track, needs to rely on fourteen spotters spaced around the big oval who are wired to his assistants on the platform. "You look for something wrong with a car. A car smoking. A pipe dragging. Or something very serious. A spin or a crash. If nothing goes wrong, you don't need me. You try to take in everything. I watch for any unusual movement in the cars. I look to see if a driver is wilting in the car. I look primarily in the fourth turn, where the cars are coming from. My helpers look into turn one. For the first couple or three laps, I'm really on edge. If they're going to get into bad trouble, that's the time."

As the cars blur past to complete the second lap, Rutherford is still five lengths to the good. Then comes Foyt. Ten more car lengths back is a bog of cars led by Johncock. Trailing him are Sneva, Carter, Dallenbach. Moving well, Parsons is eighth. As the field charges through turn one, Foyt closes the gap separating him from Rutherford. Down the backstretch, Foyt blisters along, his car clearly showing more straightaway thrust than Rutherford's, and just as they enter the third turn, Foyt ducks beneath number 2 and whirls by. As he does, though, he hits a puddle of oil dropped by another racer and his car skids rapidly up the banking, slipping, slipping, and brushes perilously close to the wall. Wrenching the wheel with all the ability he has, Foyt rescues the car. Meanwhile, Rutherford manages to flit by on the inside of Foyt, recovering the lead. He is ahead coming out of the fourth turn, and as the cars fly down the straightaway, Rutherford stays high in the groove, hard against the wall. Foyt, knowing he's got the power and unruffled by his near disaster with the concrete, dives inside to try another pass. Most other drivers would wait. Foyt wants the lead. Anything to win this race. As the cars reach the first turn, Foyt has slid by again and has the lead. Rutherford waves as Foyt goes by. A loud racket rises from the big crowd. This time, Foyt holds the car down on the inside line, smoothly negotiates the corner, then drifts up outside. He begins to stretch his advantage. At 200 miles per hour, glued to the banked turns, he is going as fast as an Indianapolis car has ever been meant to go. The race is but three laps old, and already Foyt and Rutherford are locked in an electric duel. And Johncock, Sneva, Dallenbach, Carter, and not much farther back, Parsons, Bobby Unser, and Andretti (climbing all the way from nineteenth) are running strong. Everyone figured to have a chance is showing himself.

The yellow flag. Four laps down. The car of Dick Simon, the man who didn't expect to win, has petered to a stop on the apron inside turn two. His engine failed. He will be credited with thirty-second place. The cars are slowed to 80 miles per hour, cruising speed for their monster power plants, while a wrecker lugs Simon's broken machine off the course. Drivers are to maintain their positions on the track. No passing is allowed. Eight yellow "pacer lights" wink around the track, changing numbers every few seconds, like a missile countdown. One. Two. Three. Four. And so on. If a driver is holding position, he should spot the same number on every light. If not, he is either gaining or losing ground. It is easy to beat the system. Only the driver himself really knows what number he first sees when the yellow is thrown.

During the caution period, the drivers run in a high second gear, making sure the engine revolutions are kept up, so the engine doesn't cool off. If it did, when the green flag waved and the throttle was floored, the engine would blow. Drivers take the time to study their gauges closer now, searching for signs of early trouble. If gauges start to stutter, something is wrong. The order is Foyt, Rutherford, Johncock, Sneva, Carter, Dallenbach, Andretti, Parsons. There is chatter in the crowd, the sound of a gurgling mountain stream. The fans shriek at the drivers, tell them what to do, when, and how. As Parsons passes his pit, Robin Miller hoists the pit board with "176" scribbled on it, the latest lap speed. Parsons nods.

Straggling well back of the leaders at this point is Al Unser, one of the favorites. He fell behind almost the instant the green flag was displayed. Is his engine sick? After the race, he will say that in a strategy meeting with his team it was agreed to run a conservative race for the first half of the distance, conserving fuel, then a flat-out dash, hoping to pick off cars as tanks began to dry up. The team had thought of one other tack: run all-out from the start, then pray for rain. The latter strategy will haunt them in the race's aftermath.

On the seventh lap, Simon's car safely off the track, the green comes out again. Foyt stretches his lead over Rutherford. He pours out of the fourth turn, pressing up the long straightaway at 200 miles per hour, pulling away from the cars behind him. He must be developing a murderous appetite. No driver can keep up the torrid pace of these early laps, not for four hundred and ninety more miles. The order of the trailing cars remains the same. The traffic has begun to loosen up, the field spreading itself around the complete length of the Speedway. Abruptly, on the ninth lap, Roger McCluskey, in the Lindsey Hopkins car, rated a good dark-horse threat, spins wildly in the third turn and stuffs his car into the wall in a bone-jarring collision, bending the racer. He drifts to a stop in the infield. The left-rear tire is canted out at a bizarre angle, the rear wing is crumpled like an accordion. McCluskey is groggy from the blow, but otherwise is all right. He is out of the race; Lindsey Hopkins' dream will wait another year. The yellow is tossed again, as a wrecker rumbles out to snatch up the damaged machine.

It is still early for pit stops, and Foyt and Rutherford keep lapping the track. Miller gives Parsons the okay sign as he putters past, in sixth position now, a straightaway out of the lead. Two caution laps go by, and then in a burst, Sneva, Andretti, Johncock, and Rutherford make for the pits. Rutherford is out in twelve seconds. Johncock takes twenty. A slow stop. Andretti limps in with a flat tire, punctured by debris from McCluskey's car. His stop is slower still, pushing him farther behind. Sneva comes in bleeding. A coil spring fell off McCluskey's racer when he clouted the wall. Rutherford ran over it, flinging it through the air. It crashed through Sneva's windshield, snapped the chin strap on his helmet, cut his mouth, and dropped in his lap. Dazed but able to maintain control, Sneva hurled the spring into the infield. His pit crew tapes the windshield and hands Sneva a Band-Aid. All of the crews are murmuring about handling problems brought on by the tires not giving good adhesion. The cars are running extremely loose. The crews are hopeful the problems will sort themselves out as rubber is packed down on the course.

Four caution laps have flitted by and now Foyt, in a seeming moment of indecision, abruptly blurts into the pits. Simultaneously, the green flag comes out. The stop will cost Foyt precious time, the cars now running at full speed. He hurriedly takes on fuel and darts out in just six seconds, but he still loses ground to the frontrunners who pitted under the yellow. Such is Foyt's haste to get back on the course that he leaves with a long-handled wrench lying on the side of the racer. Pad Vidan readies a black flag to send Foyt back to the pits to have it removed. Luckily, the wrench falls off in the second turn, saving Foyt from the black flag. Out comes the yellow again so a spotter can scoop the wrench off the racing surface. Foyt finds himself still in strong contention, not knuckling under to the pressure.

The pits flood with cars. Rutherford hastily pits again, taking on new tires, momentarily shoving Pancho Carter into the lead. Parsons now storms into the pits for his first stop. Deftly, the crew scrambles into action, like open-heart surgeons. Their movements braid together. Front and rear tires have been brought out, but Parsons vetoes them. Bent double, Matt Murphy fits the fuel nozzle into the tank, filling it to capacity. Reny Filiatreau slaps in the vent bottle. A fast stop. Six seconds. As Parsons screams back into the chase, Texas coddles the vent bottle in his arms and pours the excess fuel back into the fueling tank.

"That was a great stop."

"Nice—real nice stop."

"Way to go, guys. Way to go."

Lap seventeen. The green comes out. Immediately, Dallenbach blasts past Carter and seizes the lead. Johncock and Rutherford move by to take over second and third. Sneva is fifth, Foyt sixth. In a bold move, Parsons passes Foyt, hoisting himself to sixth. Smiles and applause from his crew, egging him on. Next lap, right at the starting line, Foyt bulls inside Parsons and moves ahead. Right behind Parsons are Bobby Unser and Andretti, the three of them around a straightaway behind Dallenbach in the lead. Once a race starts, you don't know where to look. There's the fight for the lead. There are the other battles for various positions throughout the field. A bunch of twelve cars thrusts down the straightaway, Dallenbach and Johncock toward the rear, trying to worm their way through, putting a lap on slower machines. They dive inside and five cars run abreast of each other down past the starting line. Traffic is thick. The crowd is on its feet, screaming wildly.

Dallenbach leaps out of the pack, lapping everyone in it but Johncock, who is close behind.

Twenty-two laps gone.

Texas: "Hanging right there with Bobby Unser."

Finley: "He's staying in the right place."

Reny: "Let's see her fly, Johnny."

With his hands shoved down in his pockets and his shoulders pushed high, Vatis watches the cars beat past.

Johncock captures the lead. He runs strong. Perhaps he can win. Rutherford is now second, and Foyt, in fifth, is beginning to slice through the pack. Parsons is eighth, cars piled up behind him. The drivers almost inevitably lose all sense of their position. Their strategy must be directed from the pits. On large blackboards, information such as "P6" (You are in sixth place) or instructions such as "EZ" (Take it easy) are flashed to the speeding drivers.

The loudspeakers: "And A. J. Foyt is moving up again on the leaders. A. J. Foyt moving up on the leaders. The leader is Gordon Johncock. Eyes now on Gordon John-cock. . . . Now A. J. Foyt right next to Wally Dallenbach on the course, going through the short chute south end of the track. . . . Just four and a half seconds separating Gordon Johncock, the race leader, and A. J. Foyt. . . . A. J. Foyt has now moved around Wally Dallenbach. A. J. Foyt has moved around Wally Dallenbach."

It seems like three-quarters of the race has passed, but it has not yet been a quarter. Foyt continues to chew up ground on the lead trio. He throws his car into the corner in a snarl of noise and dust and goes bucking into the short chute. A tremendously close race thus far. On lap twenty-seven, Foyt snatches third to a thunderclap of applause. As Parsons whirls by his pit, still eighth, he points a finger at the rear of the car. Miller looks puzzled. He gazes over at Barnes.

"Give him RR," Barnes shouts. "RR" stands for right-rear tire. Parsons might want a tire on his next stop.

Miller chalks the letters on the board and flashes it at

Parsons the next time around. Parsons wags his wrist when he sees it. The car is running loose. Tire problems.

Thirty-two laps. Thirty-three. Thirty-four. On lap thirty-five, Johncock is still the race leader and Rutherford ducks into the pits under the green. A sixteen-second stop. Then Dallenbach blunders in. The man on the right front is having trouble yanking the wheel off, forcing a slow stop of over twenty-four seconds. That will cost him roughly the length of the straightaway to Rutherford. Andretti pits, barreling in much too fast. He overshoots his assigned pit area by ten feet, then stalls the engine. His crew tugs the car back by the wing. The stop eats up over thirty seconds. Andretti's engine has begun to sour on top of his pit problems, damping the hopes of the fastest qualifier. Now Johncock and Foyt both stop, Johncock taking seventeen seconds and Foyt just thirteen. It begins to look as if the race will be written in the pits, by the air wrenches and the fuel nozzles, by the better crew.

Lap thirty-nine, and it is Rutherford in the lead. Foyt is second, then Johncock, then Parsons now in fourth. Parsons, though, has yet to make his second pit stop. Traffic amasses behind—six, seven, ten cars. Miller gives Parsons "P3" on the board, meaning pit in three laps. Parsons acknowledges the board with a nod of his head. "P2" is posted on the board, but as Miller prepares to display it, Parsons pits, two laps early.

"Heads up," Barnes shouts.

"Here he comes."

"Look out. Look out."

Frantically, the crew pours over the wall and gets to work. It is not a good idea for a driver to come in sooner than expected. A pit crew psyches itself up for a stop, adrenaline begins to rush; concentration reaches a peak when the car lurches in. An unexpected stop leaves a crew slightly disarrayed. What is he doing here now? The crew is annoyed that Parsons stopped early. Parsons is displeased with the car running so loose, wants to get new rubber. The car is jacked up. Off flies the right rear.

"Skeeereet-reeet." Parsons shakes off new right-front rubber. In the pits, every moment seems an eternity for the driver. On the track, cars shoot by at full speed and yet he sits motionless, the car chucking under him. Sixteen seconds and Parsons is out.

"Good job, Barnes," Miller shouts as Parsons storms out.

Barnes nods.

"He's running nice," Vatis says. "So far, so good. He's running that track. He's right in the thick of it."

Parsons steams by and twirls a finger around in the air. Miller looks perplexed. He writes "Boost?" on the sign board, wondering whether the turbocharger boost is set too low. He shows it to Barnes, who nods, and as Parsons comes by again, Miller wags the board at him. No response. Miller scratches it in bigger letters and flashes it again. Still nothing, though Parsons is nestled between two other cars and is busy steering. Now Miller scribbles "Loose" on the board and sticks that up. Nothing. The next time, Parsons twirls his finger again and his father hollers, "Hey, he wants the lap. He wants to know what lap he's on." His father knows Parsons' signals like a favorite tune.

"L47" is given to Parsons the next time around. The lap after that Miller gives him "174," his latest speed.

Lap fifty. A quarter of the distance. The race is an hour old. Rutherford comes out of the corner with a scream and blisters down the straight. Nine seconds pass. On comes Foyt. A few seconds later, Johncock appears. For the moment, the race has taken a formal pattern. Rutherford will set the pace. Foyt and Johncock will follow. They will not allow themselves to fall too far back. Then will come a group of others—Carter, Dallenbach, Andretti, Sneva, Parsons—still very much in the running, dancing and weaving among themselves like giant colored butterflies. Not in many years has the race been locked in so tight a battle.

On lap fifty-eight, Parsons points to the right rear.

He's unhappy with the tire, wants it changed on his next stop. Miller passes the signal to Finley. The laps pass in waves of worry and concupiscence. Parsons' crew waits uneasily, totally absorbed in watching just one car. Their faces are expressionless, their concentration complete. They look upstream into the river of fiber glass flowing toward them.

"Way to go. Way to go," Reny says. "He looks strong out there. How to drive this track."

"We got a shot, I think."

"Got to keep picking off those cars."

"Right."

"Boy, is my throat dry. Can't even spit."

"Why don't you drink some water?"

Rutherford booms past. He is running with loose, all-out, fluid abandon. His pursuers, Foyt and Johncock, are picking up some ground. Cars stream by all over the track. Hard to say who is running where. Time for pit stops soon. The crews are nervously trying the air hammers, making sure they still work. Pit boards in the air. Laps tick by.

Lap sixty. "There's a tow-in on number 92," rings the loudspeakers. Steve Krisiloff has run out of fuel on the backstretch. The crew erred in figuring his mileage. He was due in next time around. Up to now, Krisiloff had been running a steady race, working up from twenty-third starting position into the top fifteen. The error will cost him, probably drop him two or three laps farther behind the leaders. The car will have to be towed halfway around the track to be fueled up. Vatis shakes his head in disgust. Expecting a yellow, Rutherford pounds into the pits, though the green stays out. The stop is fast, but then as Rutherford steams out the yellow is dropped. A bad break. The crowd roars. Foyt jolts into the pits, gaining precious seconds on Rutherford.

Parsons peels into the pits. His third stop. Fuel is pumped in and Parsons signals for new rubber on the right side, front and back. Kneeling, Barnes vigorously begins to spin off the nut. Finley is stooped beside the right front, working the air wrench. "Skeereet-reet." Barnes finishes his tire. Finley is having problems. Frustrated, he can't get the wheel properly aligned. He's hammering at the wheel with the air wrench. Barnes scurries over to pitch in. He pounds with his fist. It is a dreadfully slow stop, softened only by the fact that it came under yellow. Forty seconds.

"Damn, that was too slow."

"We'll make it up. We'll make it up."

"It was on the yellow. It's not so bad; it was on the yellow."

Questions come to mind as the race plods on. Can Foyt run strong all day? Is Rutherford perhaps holding back? How is everyone on fuel? Fuel is power. Who will break? Who will pick up from the yellows and who won't? Rutherford must be wondering about Foyt. Can he run so fast and have fuel at the end? Have an engine at the end? Foyt is not like that. There is never fear in his mind that he will fail to win a race. If his car lives, he is confident he will outrun everyone.

"Oh, my God, look at this!"

"Look, here he is, here he is!"

"Over the wall, over the wall!"

"Oh, shit!"

Parsons creeps into the pits again. His right-front wheel is missing. The crew scrambles into action. Texas tries to jam the jack under the car. It won't fit, the right front is dragging too low. He tries the other side. No good. Covered with grease, Barnes heaves the car up with his hands. Wallowing on his knees, Finley struggles to get a fresh wheel on. The nerves of the crew are tense and growing tenser. Parsons sits in the car wall-eyed, his hands roping up around the steering wheel. Finley hadn't gotten the pins in properly the last stop, the reason the tire flew off. As soon as Parsons left the pit apron, he could feel that the car was very loose. He knew the wheel was going to come off. He was praying that he could get around to the pits first. It flew off in the second turn. Parsons is furious at Finley for his error. He could have been seriously injured, and he will certainly lose valuable time. Through his visor, he curses Finley. Finley looks up at Parsons. He can't hear a word, but he can see the anger in Parsons' eyes. Twenty-five seconds for the stop. Barnes is mad also, his face flushed. In anger, he thumps his fist hard into the tool box. "Goddamn!"

A race official stamps down to the pit. "Whoever put it on didn't get those pins in."

"I hammered the shit out of it," Finley says.

A terrible bleak feeling of loss in the pits. There's no doubt in Barnes's mind that the lost time will make it impossible for Parsons to win the race.

★★★★★★★★★★★★★★★★

The green flag waves on the sixty-fourth lap. In the exchange of pit stops, Foyt has moved back out front. The cars blast down the straight like a swarm of metal insects. The running order: Foyt, Rutherford, Johncock, Carter, Dallenbach. Parsons has fallen from the top fifteen. Foyt's lead is eleven seconds. Covering ground like a sonic boom, Foyt appears to be delivering on his promise. He seems to have a margin of speed, power that his closest pursuers lack. First to fifth place is a thirty-seven second gap, remarkably narrow for a race that is more than a quarter gone. Twenty-seven cars from the starting field are still on the racetrack, a large number, attributable to the cool weather; engines encounter less trouble in cool weather. The tire difficulties suffered by the cars earlier appear to have corrected themselves.

If you have no special interest in any of the drivers, the race by now can become tedious. It has taken a pattern. There is not a great deal of passing, except for slower cars being dropped another lap behind. Some will be lapped ten, fifteen times before the race is over. Beyond the leaders, it is impossible to tell who is running where. The racers are spaced around the course, and there is a sensation of a train passing that never seems to end. It can seem a disappointing race, especially if you aren't used to motor racing on a big track. It's the kind of race where, owing to the layout of the course, you can never see more than about a third of the action. It's the kind of race where the cars are so low and go so fast that it is difficult to pick out their numbers as they flash by. For the drivers, the race has become a matter of endurance. Stick as near the leaders as possible without unduly straining the engine. Hope the car holds together. Hope you don't crash. Fans who care about a particular car still hang on every lap, agonizing. Many other fans, particularly those in the infield, have begun to lose interest. A number of them have fallen asleep. Others have turned to different pursuits. They dance. They play poker. They drink.

Miller wags the board with "Push" written on it. It is the seventieth lap. Parsons nods. Miller shows the board to Barnes and Finley. They know the problem: When the wheel tore off, the right-front end of the car scraped along the hard asphalt, which rubbed out the narrow bumper guard on the car that blocks air from passing underneath. At speed, the guard will be almost brushing the ground. With it gone, air has begun to whoosh underneath, lifting the right front of the car and causing the car to push severely. There's nothing that can be done about it now; Parsons' lap speeds have gone down. The crew watches in mounting gloom.

Rutherford is chopping away at Foyt's lead. Foyt still has the thrust down the straightaways, but he seems to be having trouble negotiating the corners. Rutherford is noticeably quicker through the turns. Every passing lap, more and more of Foyt's lead dissolves. Eight seconds. Six seconds. Five seconds. Foyt is now the mouse, Rutherford the cat.

Foyt has come up to place a lap on Tom Sneva, though he has difficulty getting by. Sneva is making him work. Foyt is trapped behind Sneva, can't get by. His car no longer seems to be handling well. The rear end appears to be lurching out in the turns. Though clearly quicker than Sneva down the straightaway, Foyt is slower in the corners. Something is wrong with the car. Foyt is given the "+5" sign from his crew, his lead now five seconds.

The next lap it is four. Foyt's lead is steadily atrophying. Rutherford comes on and on, Foyt apparently helpless to keep him back. For the first time in a long while, Rutherford can see Foyt's car. Up till now, Foyt would be in the first corner by the time Rutherford swept out of the fourth turn. It is a psychological advantage for the second-place man to be able to see the leader. It buoys his confidence that he can catch him. Foyt has changed his groove, is driving much deeper into the turns, slamming on the brakes, then jamming the throttle, trying to get the engine revolutions back up. He has to fight the car coming out of the corners.

By the seventy-ninth lap, Foyt and Rutherford are tail to nose. Rutherford stalks Foyt, tries to pass on the inside and then swerves outside. He's driving all over Foyt, can't get him on the straights, though. Foyt must be agonizing. He knows he is going to be taken. Over his two-way radio, Foyt is telling his pit crew: "I can't hold him off anymore. I'm going to have to let him by."

Loudspeakers: "Foyt is trying to hold off Rutherford. Foyt is still leading Rutherford in the midway point of the backstretch. Foyt still leading. Foyt still leading. Rutherford cutting underneath, trying to get around him in the short chute. . . . Rutherford is leading. Rutherford is leading. Rutherford will lead going into turn number four. Rutherford is the race leader. Foyt is now second."

There is a crescendo of yawping from the crowd. Rutherford immediately stretches his advantage, peeling off from Foyt like a Jaguar taking off from a truck moving up a winding mountain road. Two car lengths. Three. Four. Ten. Worry in Foyt's pit. It looks like Rutherford has turned the race, more so with every passing lap. On the eighty-first lap, Foyt pits, takes on new right-side rubber, pushes away a proffered cup of water, steams out after fourteen seconds. He's still in second place. A fine pit stop.

The laps drone on. Foyt and his crew have begun to suspect that something has broken somewhere in the suspension, ruining the handling. The car is running extremely loose in the corners. Foyt is forty seconds back now. Yet Rutherford's crew signals for him to pit the next time around. An important stop. If it's slow, Foyt could regain the lead. On lap eighty-five, Rutherford ducks in, takes rubber on the right side, refuses a drink, pours out in fourteen point two seconds, the lead still his. Foyt is ten seconds back.

Barnes asks Parsons' father to go down to the scorer's area to see if he can find out where Parsons is running. Only the first ten cars have been announced, and Parsons is not among them. When he comes back, he tells Barnes, "John's not in the first eleven, that's all I can find out."

"Okay."

Miller gives Parsons the sign to pit in three laps, but again he blurts in two laps early. This is his fifth pit stop. Again two tires on the right side. Again Finley has trouble fitting the front tire on. Texas drops the jack.

"Nope, ain't done," Finley hollers.

The jack is raised. Barnes scampers over and finishes the job. A thirty-second stop. Terribly slow. Three laps later, Miller flashes the sign board at Parsons with "169" scratched on it. The speed keeps dipping.

Vatis checks the fuel consumption, does some hasty calculation. Mileage looks good. Better than 1.8 so far. The caution flags have kept it up.

On the ninety-first lap, another yellow. A car has stalled in turn three and will have to be towed in. At once, there is a pit flurry.

"Here he comes again," Barnes shouts.

"Hey. Hey. Heads up."

Parsons pits for another right-rear tire, trying change after change in the hope that the push in the car can be cured. Twenty-one seconds. Foyt makes a stop in sixteen seconds, trying new rubber to fix the loose condition in his car. The problems persist. The race is an hour and thirty-five minutes old.

The green on lap ninety-four. Rutherford still owns a ten-second advantage on Foyt. He has a safe lead over Johncock. A cool wind is scuttling papers along the pit wall. Dark clouds lie over the covered grandstands along the main straightaway. It is extremely humid.

The order is Rutherford, Foyt, Johncock, Carter, Dallenbach. Rutherford goes around Carter like a flicker of light, lapping him and leaving only the front three cars on the same lap. Rutherford slips through traffic as easily as sand through twitchy fingers. Now Foyt's pit crew flags the pit board with the message: "Rain 15 miles west of here." The crew is telling Foyt to stand on it, try to catch Rutherford because it may pour. The overcast skies are pressing in. A sharp wind with teeth combs through the track. It stirs up scraps and creates a funnel of newspaper that swirls up in a mad ballet. Rain seems imminent. Now the pits begin to ring with comment on the weather.

"It's gonna drizzle on us."

"Yeah, looks like rain."

"Gonna be a wet one."

"Damn, damn, damn. Don't rain. Please, don't rain."

"I can't believe this stinking weather."

The field enters the ninety-eighth lap. Foyt is desperately working to close up on Rutherford. Twice in the last three years rain has curtailed the race. Should water fall after more than half the race is completed, even if only a lap past the halfway mark, it can be declared an official race.

A hard gust of wind hits the track. Huge mosques of clouds, miles high, blow in. Then the raindrops come down. The yellow is brought out. A hundred laps are down. The cars slow their speed, make two more circuits. The weather worsens, the plash of rain increasing now. These cars can't run in rain. There are no treads on the tires; the slightest film of moisture will lift them up and they will aquaplane. Clutching an umbrella over his head, Pat Vidan wags the red flag as the hundred and second lap is completed, and the cars grumble into the pits. Fans scatter for cover and umbrellas bloom up into the bleak sky.

One by one, the cars steer into their pits, and the drivers clamber out of the machines. Crews check over the cars. Tarpaulins are draped over the racers to protect them from the rain, giving them the look of furniture in a house closed for the season.

Grimly, Parsons slides off his helmet and pats down his hair with an agitated hand. He moves over and kneels down to look at the right front of the car. His father comes over.

"Boy, that sure got beat to hell," Parsons says.

"Yeah, it sure did."

"Boy, I couldn't believe Finley did that. He's never done nothing like that."

His father pulls a dripping handkerchief out of his soaked trousers and hands it to Parsons, who mops his face and neck. Toweling his wet head, Parsons is silent for a while. His face—dark, weary, defeated, abject. There is a drop of water on the end of his nose. Mike Griffin, the scorer, comes over to show him the lap charts. He stands, drips, and listens. He pushes his seaweed hair back along the crown of his head. Wet and sozzled, his shirt clinging wet to his body, Griffin goes over the charts.

"You were running really well up till the tire went. Had you up to fourth at one point. Mostly, you were running sixth to eighth."

"Yeah, the car felt fine till that tire went. Then everybody was catching me. Jesus, cars were running 170 and going by me."

"Yeah, I know. The speeds dropped off a lot."

"How were the stops?"

"Except for the first one, they were pretty slow. One of them was forty seconds."

"Brother."

"You know where we're running?" Parsons asks.

"We couldn't find out. Not in the first ten."

"One thing for sure. We're not in this race any more."

Reny walks over. "You want something to drink?"

"Yeah, I'll have something," Parsons says. "How about a new car?"

Reny brings back a cardboard box full of Cokes and hands them out to the crew. The crewmen perch on the wall, listening to the splash and beat of the rain. The race has gone enough laps, just barely enough laps, to be called official if the weather doesn't improve. It would be the shortest 500 in history.

The stopping of the race allows Foyt's crew to go over his car, and they find that the front swaybar, a steel arm that stabilizes the car through the turns and keeps it from rolling over, has cracked, bringing on the handling problem. Foyt could have finished the race with the broken sway bar, but he probably wouldn't have caught Rutherford. Now, during the delay, repairs are allowed and a new sway bar is installed. Meanwhile, Foyt sends a crewman to complain to race officials that Rutherford picked up time on him during the yellow-flag periods, cutting nineteen seconds off his lead at one point. Rutherford denies the charge, maintaining he was simply keeping up with the field and that Foyt forgot he made five pit stops to his four. The scorers find no discrepancy.

The drivers and crews sit around in the pits, watching the rain make big puddles. Then many drift down to the garages, where some drivers play hearts, others play golf with a couple of brooms and some baseballs. One mechanic is pacing up and down the garage, slapping his fist into his hand and muttering, "Stop the rain, stop the rain, let's get this miserable race going."

After a time, a new loop of weather blows in. The drizzle stops and the ragged clouds disperse out over the grandstands. The day brightens and warms. The sun comes out. The concrete steams. It looks like the track may be dried and the race resumed. Tow trucks, water wagons, and a tremendous metal blower trundle onto the track and begins to lap it, drying the asphalt with their treads.

Two and a half hours pass. Officials peer at the track surface. A voice comes over the loudspeakers: "All drivers report to your cars. We're going to get a lineup for a restart. Drivers report to your cars." A full-throated roar breaks out from the huge crowd. The cars are shoved into the restart order down the pit apron, one behind the other, frog fashion. Crews and drivers collect around the machines. But clouds begin to pack up again, the sun is gone. Rain pebbles down, then thunks steadily on the pavement. Tarpaulins go back over the cars.

A newscaster bends over to talk to Foyt, half-wedged in his car. He says, "A. J., over the years they've always said you were very lucky—"

"Well, I'm not very lucky today," Foyt says. "You know, it's just a shame. The race could have been started thirty minutes ago, and they just mess around and mess around. It's just, you know, a bad deal. . . . You know, it's a hell of a note to be running the way we have been the last two years and can't win the thing. . . . Maybe we're not supposed to win. . . . This is very disgusting and disappointing."

His racing cap angled on his head, Foyt wiggles out of the car and starts pacing up and down the line of cars, simmering like a caged tiger. He feels certain that if the race were to resume he would win it all. The announcement crackles over the loudspeakers: "It's raining very heavily now, and there would be no way we could dry the track. It would take at least two or three hours. So the 1976 winner is Johnny Rutherford. For the second time, Johnny Rutherford is the winner of the Indianapolis 500."

Foyt is officially placed second, followed by Johncock,

Dallenbach, Carter, and Sneva. Al Unser is awarded seventh. Andretti ran eighth. Playboy Salt Walther was ninth. Bobby Unser, the defending champion, came in tenth. After starting dead last, Jan Opperman finished sixteenth.

Fans begin to stream toward the exit gates. Many push their way toward Gasoline Alley and Victory Lane. Somebody in the stands, way up high, is blowing into some kind of air horn. Some people snoring it off in the infield don't know the race is over, don't know who won, don't care. Rutherford's car is rolled amid a garland of flowers to where the 500 Festival Queen awaits. A local schoolteacher lugs the eighty-pound Borg-Warner Trophy the hundred yards from the starting line to Victory Lane. Another tradition, he's done it for twenty-six years; months before the race, he starts training to get in shape to carry the weight of the trophy. Rutherford is handed the traditional bottle of cold milk. As he drinks it, a wreath is draped over his neck. He grins at a battery of cameras. His attractive, blond wife is shaking with excitement. Others—family, friends, officials, car owners, mechanics—arrive to be photographed with the winners, car and man. Rutherford has won a total of two hundred and fifty-five thousand dollars for an hour and forty-three minutes of racing, two thousand four hundred and seventy-five dollars a minute.

The other crews plod back to the garages. "I feel like ten pounds of manure in a five-pound bag, that's what I feel like," a soggy crewman says. "We were just starting to run. Just starting to stitch."

"I feel so low I could sink in a glass of water," a mechanic says.

Johnny Parsons has already returned to garage 65, sheltering himself from the rain. The rest of the crew drifts in now, pushing the two race cars. Vatis straggles in, water dripping from his hair. Friends begin to gather. The garage is solemn. Vatis fidgets a lot, trying to smile gamely. "Do you know what our final positions are?" he asks.

"Parsons got twelfth."

"And Krisiloff?"

"Twenty-fourth."

"Mm," he says. He goes over to the refrigerator and picks out a beer.

Parsons grabs hold of a mop and swishes water off the garage floor. Then he sits down on a folding chair. He stares ahead like a child. Finley shuffles over and apologizes for his mistake. Parsons nods. The radio is on, and in a matter-of-fact voice, Johnny Rutherford is delivering his Victory Lane speech. He says, "Racing is funny. Sometimes it works for you and sometimes it doesn't. This time it worked for us. Early in the race, we had some handling problems. At our second pit stop, we changed the right-side tires and my car seemed to come to life. I have mixed emotions. I would have liked it to be sunny and to race A. J. to the finish, but I also savor the win . . . I feel sad for A. J. This is sort of a hollow victory, but I'll take it. Victory is sweet, however you get it. I'd rather be lucky than good."

Every driver shares in the purse. Parsons' car will get twenty-five thousand dollars. The share for Krisiloff's car will be sixteen thousand.

Bob Bunting draws a breath. "It's a bad way to end a race like this. All this work and all these people come, then you go half the distance."

"One thing you can't figure—that's the weather."

"There's probably not a man here happy, not even Rutherford. This ain't no way you want to win a race."

"I ran good before the tire went," Parsons says. The top half of his uniform is knotted at his waist. "We smoked off some good cars. We could have run up there a long, long time."

Vatis is not paying attention. "I know we could have done better. It was a series of goof-ups. We beat ourselves.

I really think we could have upped our positions if they ran the rest of the race. I'm almost certain we could have gotten top ten, maybe top five."

Cigarette smoke is billowing out of Finley's mouth. "It's real disappointing. We could have run better."

He looks at the car.

"The car don't know it lost, at least. That's something. It don't know it lost."

Slouched on the floor, his T-shirt greased and soggy, Barnes splits open a can of beer. He sips some, mops his moustache with the back of his arm. He looks washed out. He is in a brooding mood. Rain patters down again outside. "It's like the whole year shot to hell. We could have done better. We looked very amateurish. We could never get our act together. If we hadn't lost the wheel, you can't tell how we would have done. We were sixth when we lost that wheel. I'll be rerunning this race and rerunning this race for weeks."

Reny says, "It's damn disappointing. This big-time auto racing is damn disappointing. It really is. You don't like to end one like this."

"We didn't give it enough. We're made of better than this. We just didn't get the breaks."

"That's part of racing."

There are crowds outside in the alley, swarming by, prowling for autographs, for gossip. Anyone is allowed through the gates now. People are drunk, people are greeting one another. There is whistling and people waving to one another. The rain is heavy, smacking hard against the roofs of the garages. There is lots of conversation. Everyone is drinking and talking in the timeless aftermath of the race.

There is laughter around the car now, shot through with moments of high-pitched intensity. Sandwiches are being pulled from a large paper bag, more beer handed around. The garage is full of people. Parsons moves about with the sandwich bag coddled in his arm. "Who wants a sandwich? Who wants a delicious sandwich?" Shorty flicks on the radio for some music, drowning out the rain clattering outside. A ballad about a taxi driver falls from the speakers.

Butch says, "I didn't think we'd win, but I sure didn't expect that many cars to beat us."

"It's a real letdown, but it's all over now."

"I just wish it hadn't rained," Parsons say. "With half a race more, we could have got to the top five, made something of the race. Up till that wheel went, things were looking good. We could run with almost everyone. It'll take a few weeks to get over this. It's depressing. I wish the wheel hadn't come off."

INDIANAPOLIS 500 WINNERS

Year	Winner	Time	MPH
1911	Ray Harroun	6:42:08.00	74.590
1912	Joe Dawson	6:21:06.00	78.720
1913	Jules Goux	6:35:05.00	75.930
1914	Rene Thomas	6:03:45.00	82.470
1915	Ralph DePalma	5:33:55.51	89.840
1916	Dario Resta*	3:34:17.00	84.000
1919	Howard Wilcox	5:40:42.87	88.050
1920	Gaston Chevrolet	5:38:32.00	88.620
1921	Tommy Milton	5:34:44.65	89.620
1922	Jimmy Murphy	5:17:30.79	94.480
1923	Tommy Milton	5:29:50.17	90.950
1924	L. L. Corum and Joe Boyer	5:05:23.51	98.230
1925	Peter DePaolo	4:56:39.46	101.130
1926	Frank Lockhart†	4:10:14.95	95.904
1927	George Souders	5:07:33.08	97.545
1928	Louis Meyer	5:01:33.75	99.482
1929	Ray Keech	5:07:25.42	97.585
1930	Billy Arnold	4:58:39.72	100.448
1931	Louis Schneider	5:10:27.93	96.629
1932	Fred Frame	4:48:03.79	104.144
1933	Louis Meyer	4:48:00.75	104.162
1934	William Cummings	4:46:05.20	104.863

*1916—300 Miles (Scheduled)
†1926—400 Miles (Rain)

Year	Winner	Time	MPH
1935	Kelly Petillo	4:42:22.71	106.240
1936	Louis Meyer	4:35:03.39	109.069
1937	Wilbur Shaw	4:24:07.80	113.580
1938	Floyd Roberts	4:15:58.40	117.200
1939	Wilbur Shaw	4:20:47.39	115.035
1940	Wilbur Shaw	4:22:31.17	114.277
1941	Floyd Davis and Mauri Rose	4:20:36.24	115.117
1946	George Robson	4:21:26.70	114.820
1947	Mauri Rose	4:17:52.17	116.338
1948	Mauri Rose	4:10:23.33	119.814
1949	Bill Holland	4:07:15.97	121.237
1950	Johnnie Parsons*	2:46:55.97	124.002
1951	Lee Wallard	3:57:38.05	126.224
1952	Troy Ruttman	3:52:41.88	128.922
1953	Bill Vukovich	3:53:01.69	128.740
1954	Bill Vukovich	3:49:17.27	130.840
1955	Bob Sweikert	3:53:59.53	128.209
1956	Pat Flaherty	3:53:28.84	128.490
1957	Sam Hanks	3:41:14.25	135.601
1958	Jim Bryan	3:44:13.80	133.791
1959	Rodger Ward	3:40:49.20	135.857
1960	Jim Rathmann	3:36:11.36	138.767
1961	A. J. Foyt	3:35:37.49	139.130
1962	Rodger Ward	3:33:50.33	140.293
1963	Parnelli Jones	3:29:35.40	143.137
1964	A. J. Foyt	3:23:35.83	147.350
1965	Jim Clark	3:19:05.34	150.686
1966	Graham Hill	3:27:52.53	144.317
1967	A. J. Foyt	3:18:24.22	151.207
1968	Bobby Unser	3:16:13.76	152.882
1969	Mario Andretti	3:11:14.71	156.867
1970	Al Unser	3:12:37.04	155.749
1971	Al Unser	3:10:11.56	157.735
1972	Mark Donohue	3:04:05.54	162.962
1973	Gordon Johncock†	2:05:26.59	159.036
1974	Johnny Rutherford‡	3:09:10.06	158.589
1975	Bobby Unser	2:54:55.08	149.213
1976	Johnny Rutherford**	1:42:52.48	148.725

*1950—345 Miles (Rain)
†1973—332½ Miles (Rain)
‡1975—435 Miles (Rain)
**1976—255 Miles (Rain)

OFFICIAL INDIANAPOLIS MOTOR SPEEDWAY RECORDS

LAPS	MILES	TIME	MPH	DRIVER	YEAR
1	2.5	45.21	199.071	Johnny Rutherford	1973
4	10.0	3:01.44	198.413	Johnny Rutherford	1973
200	500.0	3:04:05.54	162.962	Mark Donohue	1972

1911: Ray Harroun winning the first Indianapolis 500. *Photo courtesy Indianapolis Motor Speedway.*

1912: Ralph DePalma pushes his disabled Mercedes down the front stretch; he was leading by ten miles with three laps to go when misfortune struck. *Photo courtesy Indianapolis Motor Speedway.*

The Indianapolis Motor Speedway today: Museum is large white building in infield, with golf course behind it; Gasoline Alley comprises two long sheds on left side of infield, at right angle to pit

apron; grandstands run outside left half of track. *Photo courtesy Indianapolis Motor Speedway.*

Pat Vidan with his flags. *Photo courtesy Indianapolis Motor Speedway.*

Anton "Tony" Hulman, Jr., current owner of the Speedway. *Photo courtesy Indianapolis Motor Speedway.*

The view up Gasoline Alley on a practice day. *Photo courtesy Indianapolis Motor Speedway.*

A. J. Foyt. *Photo courtesy Indianapolis Motor Speedway.*

Johnny Rutherford. *Photo courtesy Indianapolis Motor Speedway.*

Al Unser. *Photo courtesy Indianapolis Motor Speedway.*

Jan Opperman. *Photo courtesy Indianapolis Motor Speedway.*

Johnny Parsons. *Photo courtesy Indianapolis Motor Speed-way.*

In the garage, working on Number 93. Left to right: Bill Finley, John Barnes, Butch Meyer, and Mike Herion. *Photo by Bob Goshert.*

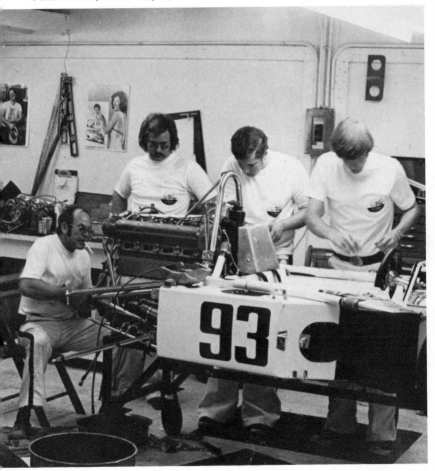

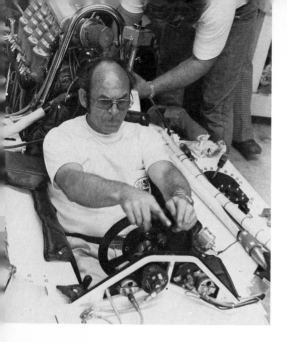

Bill Finley tests the controls of Number 93. *Photo by Bob Goshert.*

Johnny Parsons, Steve Krisiloff (driver of the second team car), and John Barnes consulting during a practice session. *Photo courtesy Indianapolis Motor Speedway.*

The start of the 1976 Indy 500. *Photo courtesy Indianapolis Motor Speedway.*

The crowd inside the first turn, commonly referred to as "the snake pit." *Photo by Enrico Ferorelli for* Sports Illustrated © *Time Inc.*

Action in the pits, with Johnny Rutherford's car in the fore-
ground. Position pole shows him leading at the time, with
Parsons running fourteenth. *Photo by Neil Leifer for* Sports
Illustrated © *Time Inc.*

Johnny Parsons heading for the pits minus his right front wheel
. . . which continues down the back stretch. *Photos by Bob
Goshert.*

Johnny Rutherford in Victory Lane. *Photo courtesy Indianapolis Motor Speedway.*